Published by ScruffyRed Press

Kilmarnock

www.scruffyred.com

The right of Iain McKie to be identified as the author of this work, has been asserted by him in accordance with the Copyright, Designs and Patent Act, 1988. ©Iain McKie 2017

ISBN: 978-0-244-93237-4

All rights reserved. No part of this publication may be reproduced, stored in a retrieval system, or transmitted in any other form or by any other means, electronic, mechanical, photocopying, recording or otherwise without prior permission of the publishers. This book may not be lent, hired out, resold or otherwise disposed of by way of trade in any form of binding or cover other than that in which it is published, without the prior consent of the publishers.

Designed and typeset by ScruffyRed.com

To contact the author: -

caminoiain@gmail.com

Version: November 30, 2017 7:11 PM

## Foreword

Inside these pages, you will find a story that you may be able to relate to. It's about a person who, like many people, faced many of life's questions and did not know the answers until he decided to face his fears and embark on a journey of a lifetime. An adventure that took him through northern Spain and into a world that is steeped in thousands of years of history, determention, heartache and love.

Where are you in your life? What is your purpose? How and when can you find happiness? Or have you already completed this journey and understand the amazing effects the Camino has on you and want to remember the places seen and feelings felt.

I wrote this book as I wanted to share my experience of walking the Camino de Santiago through the challenges of where to start with what equipment to pack and preparation done (or didn't do in some cases) to the daily adventure of walking the Camino with the importance of believing in yourself, facing your fears and embracing this physical, mental and spiritual journey.

Each day gives an insight of how my mind and actions change, learn and adapt to the Camino and life. I talk about the places visited along the way plus the incredible people that not only inspired but also became lifelong friends.

With each chapter you read you will be able to sense how you can face the fears you may have in life and understand that you have within you the ability to take on life and deliver happiness to yourself and others. Maybe you will be inspired to walk your Camino one day. So, turn the page and start the adventure.

## Acknowledgements

I would like to thank John Grant from Scruffy Red publications who, without his support, knowledge and kindness I would not have known how to even start publishing this book. My sister Angela Nicol who spent many an hour helping me dot the t's and cross the I's. My dad who over my entire life has always been there and was excited and supportive throughout my entire Camino Dream and writing this book. My beautiful Donna who daily reminds me how life is great and an eternal thank you to every person I met on the Camino who I will be forever thankful from the bottom of my heart for the hours of chat, support and love they gave so naturally.

*Buen Camino*

# Chapters

Chapter 1 – Why the Camino ..................................9
22nd January ........................................................9
23 January ..........................................................11
24th January .......................................................13
25th January .......................................................15
26 January ..........................................................17
26 January ..........................................................19
27 January ..........................................................20
28 January ..........................................................23
29th January .......................................................25
30th January .......................................................27
31st January ........................................................29
1st February ........................................................31
2nd February ......................................................34
3rd February .......................................................36
4th February .......................................................39
5th February .......................................................41
6th February .......................................................44
7th February .......................................................46
8th February .......................................................49
9th February .......................................................51
10th February .....................................................52
12th February .....................................................54
13th February .....................................................58
14th February .....................................................61

15th February ..................................................................... 63
16th February ..................................................................... 65
17th February ..................................................................... 67
18th February ..................................................................... 69
19th February ..................................................................... 72
20th February ..................................................................... 75
21st February ...................................................................... 78
22nd February .................................................................... 80
23rd February ..................................................................... 82
Chapter 2 – My journey on the Camino ............................... 85
24th February ..................................................................... 85
25th February ..................................................................... 90
Day 1, 26th February ......................................................... 96
Day 2 ................................................................................. 101
Day 3 ................................................................................. 108
Day 4 ................................................................................. 112
Day 5 ................................................................................. 119
Day 6 ................................................................................. 126
Day 7 ................................................................................. 132
Day 8 ................................................................................. 138
Day 9 ................................................................................. 144
Day 10 ............................................................................... 151
Day 11 ............................................................................... 160
Day 12 ............................................................................... 166
Day 13 ............................................................................... 172
Day 14 ............................................................................... 177

| | |
|---|---|
| Day 15 | 183 |
| Day 16 | 188 |
| Day 17 | 194 |
| Day 18 | 200 |
| Day 19 | 206 |
| Day 20 | 214 |
| Day 21 | 220 |
| Day 22 | 227 |
| Day 23 | 233 |
| Day 24 | 239 |
| Day 25 | 246 |
| Day 26 | 252 |
| Day 27 | 260 |
| Day 28 | 264 |
| Day 29 | 270 |
| Day 30 | 275 |
| Day 31 | 284 |
| Day 32 | 290 |
| Day 33 | 298 |
| Day 34 | 304 |
| Day 35 | 310 |
| Day 36 | 315 |
| 2nd April | 323 |
| 3rd April | 327 |
| 4th April | 331 |
| To finish | 335 |

# Chapter 1 — Why the Camino

## 22nd January

### Why the Camino

I ask myself the question why do I want to walk the Camino de Santiago daily yet still cannot give myself a clear answer. I just feel it. That feeling of not being able to put your finger on it or it's at the tip of your tongue. You know but it's hard to describe. A million different thoughts entwine in such a way that to even describe one of them would be a miracle worth its very own pilgrimage.

So how did I get here? here being writing the first entry of a blog to which I know not the end nor where this journey will take me. Where did this calling, as it kind of feels like that, come from or is it just the fact that I turned 44 two days ago and it's been at the back of my mind that I have a midlife crisis about to encapsulate me.

My curiosity was sparked from what I remember by the book The Pilgrimage by Paulo Coelho. I had ordered it last summer and this in turn led me to look at the Camino now and then on the internet and day dream of setting of on a five hundred mile walk to, well as I said, who knows. I say that yet have still to read past the first chapter of the book. Another spark to my interest in the Camino was I met a girl, randomly, who worked in a hotel I was staying at and somehow got into a conversation where she had told me that she had completed the Camino Frances, which translates into The French Way, the year before. She talked in a way that only intrigued me more. My mind was racing. Why was the scallop shell Hannah had given me always at the bottom of my bed spreading its shell-like glory every morning as if to say, "look at me, I'm a sign to say go and do this pilgrimage". Was it a sign? After all the scallop shell is the symbol of the Camino and from what I understand helps pilgrims find their way to Santiago de Compostela. I can't help but think that in some way that only the universe knows why my shell was handed to me many months ago on a beach in the north of Scotland and right there my journey to Santiago started.

So here I am still wondering if I'm going to do this but deep down know I am. Why else would a rucksack have arrived and clothing articles ordered, maps on the way and books being read, blog set up and people close to me hinted at that I may do this. May? My mind's laughing saying no you'll be back by May.

I will put one foot in front of the other and see where this goes. All I know is my brain is racing and I have things to do to make this happen by the end of February.

# 23 January

## Emotions and reality

Last night when I went to sleep I started thinking of the Camino and before I knew it a feeling of "do I really want to do this" slowly and tightly started to wrap itself around me. I thought of pops and thought I'll miss him, I hope he will be ok! Not a nice feeling then I started thinking that four to five weeks walking is going to be hard. Yes, it's going to be tough. Not just the walking but all the things about where to stay and eat and fill your water bottle, what about the weather and then there is the cost and the list seemed endless. I felt quite overwhelmed with fear and self-doubt. Could I could even pack a rucksack? I tossed and turned knowing that a sleep can always help my brain do what it needs to do and that I'd wake up a bit clearer.

The day was spent with reading the what to do before you walk the Camino book. A whole book dedicated to what to do before you leave. How can this be? A whole book when all you hear is you need two pairs of boxer shorts, a pair of socks, a smile and the scallop shell to hang on your perfectly fitting rucksack. It is interesting and while reading the book many of my fearful questions from last night were starting to get answered. The places to stay are cheap and plenty, there is fresh water in every village that you can use, the mileage was doable and build in a couple of rest days. Pops will be fine as I was away longer last summer and if you need the toilet while walking you just bury it. Yeh my mind was back on track. I can do this! Nothing will stop me! Next stop Paris on my way to.......... Wait I can't. As I turned the page the headline word sprung out at me like one of those toy Jack in the Box' that gave you a fright and you never found in anyway amusing. PASSPORT. Shit! My passport is out of date this year. I thought hard and remembered that come July it was no longer valid. If I was doing this walk or not I still needed to renew my passport. I was online and paying the fee the minute I finished my dinner. Two photos to get Monday and get it sent off. It takes 3 weeks to get my new passport so I should be ok for a March start. Heart racing with both excitement and fear. I think I may go through the yes and no, elation and fear, do and don't many times before I even make the decision to go or not go. That's it I'm going. I'm glad I read the book or part of as I'd have not thought about the passport. Tomorrow I will read more and get my head around this.

# 24th January
## A little at a time

As I was at work all day and had finished my Camino how to pack book I spent most of the day thinking of various Camino things. The main thing being this my place of work was a temporary job only over the festive period and January sales so I only have two working days left. The others I work with are on the same contracts and are also finishing so the common question is what are you going to do next. As I have said before I can only say that I am thinking of doing the Camino, so to my colleagues/friends I said I may go for a walk. The first people outside my close friends Donna, Junie and my pops I've said anything to. This blog has not been given to anyone so if you're reading this it's because I've booked to go and sent the link out. If you are reading this today then hello and how did you find this? Anyway, I said I was thinking of doing the Camino and gave a brief overview of what it was to those who seemed a little interested then moved on. Telling people I'm thinking about it is a bit of a deal as I know I'm going to do it but want to make sure a few things over the next few weeks fall into place e.g. my passport, my walking and my foot which is a little sore and growing a set of balls to go do it before I say to my friends I'm going. I have a fear of saying something then it falls through. It won't though.

Equipment wise I have spent the most I have ever spent on socks. I bought the 1000-mile fusion socks that guarantee no blisters. I don't believe that but they have a good name so I bought three pairs. They had better last me a few years after paying so much. These sensational socks are sold in three colours with one being fuchsia which were sold out. I liked their brightness however brown and navy will travel the Camino with me. Underwear is another journey I'm going on and will update when I have chosen. That's not the best reading but I do need some quality undies.

Tonight, I got some things ready for the volunteer radio show Perpetual Dreams I produce and present for Dunoon Community Radio. Another thing I need to think about covering while I am away. I wonder if I can do a show when I return from my pilgrimage?

# 25th January

*Just do it – so Nike said*

When I went to bed last night, as usual my head was racing at various things I should try and do when it struck me that I needed to get a guide. Kind of important I thought and had read in the packing book about one particular guide that was meant to be good so I went on a search to find it and managed to order it. It's called "what the hell am I doing this for but hey ho let's give it a bash" well of course it's not but not a bad way to look at some things. So, the guide is on its way and it's by John Brierley and called "A pilgrim's guide to the Camino de Santiago."

So how was I going to get to the start point of St Jean in southern France. I had looked firstly at getting a bus from Glasgow to Paris as it was £30, then getting the train from Paris to Bayonne at around £70 and then the short trip to St Jean. Thinking of ensuring my budget was kept low I thought that the two days to get there would be worth it to save some money and I could enjoy the view. I had previously looked at a flight to Paris which was a little more expensive and had reasoned that the extra few pounds were worth it rather than getting the bus. Mmm dilemma! Then it came back to me that there was an airport that pilgrims used to go to St Jean and I called on my old pal Google McGoogleson to search. Biarritz was the airport and with another quick search a low budget airline not only flew there but flew from Glasgow to London then on to Biarritz. A quick check of the prices and I went to sleep wondering if I should just do it.

## 26 January

*My Camino is on — I'm going*

I woke this morning with a strong urge of if you keep thinking about this then that's what you'll do just keep thinking about it. I thought of my favourite quote by Teddy Roosevelt "The man in the arena" about daring greatly and being the man in the arena. My fingers danced across my iPad not knowing if it was excitement or fear that if I did press the confirm flights button then there was more doing as well as a lot of thinking and planning to be done. The flights are booked and I leave on Wednesday 24th Feb. My Camino is on.

"It is not the critic who counts; not the man who points out how the strong man stumbles, or where the doer of deeds could have done them better. The credit belongs to the man who is actually in the arena, whose face is marred by dust and sweat and blood; who strives valiantly; who errs, who comes short again and again, because there is no effort without error and shortcoming; but who does actually strive to do the deeds; who knows great enthusiasms, the great devotions; who spends himself in a worthy cause; who at the best knows in the end the triumph of high achievement, and who at the worst, if he fails, at least fails while daring greatly, so that his place shall never be with those cold and timid souls who neither know victory nor defeat."

Excerpt from the speech "Citizenship in a Republic" delivered at the Sorbonne, in Paris, France on 23 April 1910, Theodore Roosevelt

# 26 January

## Oh and there is fitness

There is also the question of a certain level of fitness. While I walk fairly often, in the better weather, I have 4 weeks to work up to a decent mileage each day with, eventually, my rucksack and gear so I know what it feels like.

Today I walked about 4.5 miles however it was not the mileage I was thinking about but weather the waterproof gear I had bought lived up to what it says it was and as it was storming bad today it was a good chance to test it. Well it did however I learned that fleece type gloves are no good on the wet, at around 8c I was sweating into my new lightweight quick drying top and that good underwear will be required for future longer walks or there will be a sore leg where the "rucksack" rubs. I'm also doing core work daily and yoga and stretching which I've been at for a couple of months. Four weeks to increase walking fitness so I think I have time.

# 27 January

## Set up base camp

I arrived downstairs after a lovely long stay in bed and completing day twenty six of the thirty-day core challenge I had set myself. Planks are a killer however twenty-six days later I am better by a long way than on day one. I read somewhere that working on your core strength was good for walking so I am doing it. I can't see any non-benefit for it.

Walking into the kitchen there was a small package for me. As I couldn't remember what I had ordered recently there has been a few things and this was small I did have a tinge of excitement as to what it could be. Opening it up I smiled. My Camino map. This was not just any map. This map was for pops. This piece of paper with yellow dots and yellow footprints on it showed The Way. It was the centre piece of base camp. Base camp on the dining room table. The central area. The place where big decisions are made, where pops will have people gathered round showing them where I am and controlling the scene like a well-versed general showing his officers the next plan of attack.

When the map was opened for the first time I found myself trying to pronounce the names of the towns and trying to figure out what the key for the symbols were. Then I actually thought this and I regretfully quote "why didn't they send me a map in English, this is all Spanish" as quick as the thought had entered my mind I had realised my complete idiocy. I believe my next thought to myself was "Iain you are an absolute idiot" and I had a chuckle at myself.

With base camp started it was time to get the boots on and get some more miles in. Deciding that as I had not walked a lot over the winter it would be a staged increase over the next four weeks (oh man I fly four weeks today).

My rucksack is going to be around the 10kg or less mark when I do the walk. I put on my rucksack with only my waterproof trousers and jacket in it and it came to 2kg. I thought to myself. Now I get what the girl in the how to pack book was saying about every gram counts in the weight of your gear. Off I set and introduced the start of the hills and walked over the back hills of where I live. It was a beautiful walk and I was listening to the Alchemist which was the first Paulo Coelho book I had read. Well I didn't really listen, I was looking about and taking in the view of the hills and dreaming of the journey to come. A song by Coldplay came on and I was thinking about what I would feel like if, when, I complete the journey and a combination of the music and this thought unleashed some deep hidden emotion of fear entwined with joy, and yes, a few tears fell down my face and into the open space of my mouth which was being guarded by a ridiculously large smile. What would I think about when I was walking I thought....... love, addiction, depression, the power of friendship, positivity......... I was doing that anyway.

Back to our map. I loved that pilgrimsupplies.org sent a hand signed note with it. They donate all their profits to first aid support for pilgrims and Mary's meals. They also sent some flower seeds. The seeds made me think of the seed that was planted in my mind about this journey. It didn't start to grow for a while but now it's reaching for the sky.

# 28 January

## You need to get a good sleep

That feeling when you hear the post and you're waiting for something is great. Lying in bed reading my newly arrived Camino Guide the doorbell rang. Running down stairs and through the glass door I see the postman getting into his van while at the same time noticing the card on the floor. I assumed the card was stating that he had my parcel and there was no one at home so pick it up at the post office. Grabbing the card and flinging the door open waving my arms and smiling at the postman he drove off without a glance in my direction. My heart sank then I was kind of glad he had drove off realising I was now standing on the doorstep with only my boxer shorts on. Retreating inside noting that the card said the package had arrived and was in the garage I flung some trousers on to go to the garage which makes no sense after the situation at the doorstep and found the second parcel of the day. Three pairs of 1000-mile socks which pops found funny when he said, "but I thought it was five hundred miles you were walking" with a chuckle. Excited like a fat kid in a sweet shop I dived in and tried the socks on. Comfy and tight. Guaranteed no blisters. I knew there and then I'd have these blissful garments on my feet as often as the boots were on. Venturing downstairs to find yet another package the old brain was saying "this planning is fun."

I unrolled the package to see a wave of comfiness splash and dance across the floor. The travelling bed of dreams had arrived. The Highlander Echo 250, I think it's called, was there and the red and black sleeping bag was inviting me inside to try the silky warmth that would ensure perfect sleep on my journey. This is when a lesson was learned. I'm going to struggle getting used to sleeping like a mummy. Within seconds the smile was gone and hopes of really warm and comfy nights were flowing away as it felt like every night would be my own impression of an out-of-date hot tamale. I had to be able to open this coffin of sleep to get any sort of rest I thought.

No walking today as I had a guest, however I did do my weekly yoga class where the girl who teaches it has put together a sequence for walkers. Back to walking as soon as I can and more planning.

# 29th January
## Believe in your dreams

Today was a short four mile walk however it flung up a sudden down pour and high wind so I was testing myself at how quickly I could get into my waterproofs which I done in quite a quick time. No major wetness. I bought some new but cheap headphones as a bit of music when walking can be nice. An idea came to mind that I'd ask friends to tell me a song that meant something to them then download it for when walking the Camino. That way I could listen to the words and wonder why it means so much to them or they could tell me and I could maybe feel why with them as I walked. The idea was dancing about as a good idea due to the fact it could give me memories of them also.

The 1000-mile socks are now 996-mile socks after the four miles and they felt comfy however the test will be over greater distances and time. Other Camino actions tonight were eventually buying the walking underwear. There is a crazy amount of info on boxer shorts and after about an hour of reading the option of Under Armour ones were purchased. Three pairs that should protect and help areas of my body breath and stay cool. The waterproof document pouch/bag was purchased although this proved harder to do than it should have been as eventually I realised I was over analysing the waterproof fastening system of cheap highly inflated pieces of plastic. Bed bug info was scrutinised and I read and re-read and still could not figure out the stuff you're meant to put on a sheet to take with you and your gear to help prevent bed bugs. Excuse the pun but the lack of straightforward info on this was well bugging me. Moving on with the notion to come back to the bed bug issue the next items to look at were first aid items. There is a lot of info out there and with the original checklist and another printed the items will be purchased this week with the view of minimum amount of weight to carry but still with the essentials if anything was required first aid wise. Foot cream was looked at which again was confusing as to what was best so I'll revisit that however that inspired me to consider getting a pedicure. Never had one so using this as an excuse to pamper I mean have my feet looked at. So, the night was spent covering the World Wide Web wondering if I should take a Swiss Army Knife and other things that may just be weight.

> *"Dream lofty dreams, and as you dream, so you shall become. Your vision is the promise of what you shall one day be; your ideal is the prophecy of what you shall at last unveil." ~ James Allen*

# 30th January
## Every day something new

In terms of preparation this was a quiet day that was made up of mostly reading the guide book in the morning. It seems that this one is telling me that some items are ok to take that the other one said no so I'm still going with the weight is everything and trying to keep things to a minimum. First Aid basic items were bought so I have some of my first aid pack which will be pretty small but enough to get to a village if required to get more or treatment if needed. Antiseptic wipes, antiseptic cream, plasters, Compeed and dressings. A couple of other things to get that's on the checklist.

The afternoon was spent eating a lot of food and sleeping. Not the best training however obviously needed. Back to the guide book and it promotes the use of walking poles and I've read others who swear by them and others who don't. I had decided that I didn't need any but the pros for them are good while the only con for me is weight. They can be around 0.5kg which doesn't sound a lot but it will be if I don't use them. I'll sleep on it as that usually helps.

Spoke to my sister Angela who lives in Dubai on Skype tonight who didn't know I was doing this so I'm glad she does now.

Skype and these types of things are just great when people are far away. I wonder if I'll be able to Skype pops when away the odd time?

I finish my job tomorrow and join again the masses of unemployed. Part of the reason I chose to do the Camino now was I knew that I would have the time to possibly figure out what I really want to do. A question I have asked myself often however an answer still eludes me. I don't expect the answer and if I'm honest it was just good timing to walk now.

> "Somebody should tell us, right at the start of our lives, that we are dying. Then we might live life to the limit, every minute of every day. Do it! I say. Whatever you want to do, do it now! There are only so many tomorrow's." ~ Pope Paul VI

# 31st January
## A trip to the poles

A short post as I'm tired. I seem to spend more time awake at night now thinking and planning this walk. More items ordered today with the exciting, for me, purchase of walking poles. Exciting why? Because I've never used them and they are meant to be good. I'm easily pleased and my pops has said he will buy them as a gift for my journey which is lovely. I also bought some shorts and another base layer. I read more of the guide which is good as the maps make more sense. Every little bit of knowledge makes it that bit more exciting but also raises more questions in my mind.

No walking today however did finish the thirty-day challenge for core and start another one for squats starting tomorrow that's on Fatty McFattersons on Facebook. Should help a little but also fun to do it with others.

That's about all other than looking at flights for the return and exchange rates so I can budget. I asked a friend for a song they liked today so I can take it on the walk and it will remind me of them and I hope to get a few songs of some people for that reason. That friend also inspired me with their bravery in their life. I'm looking forward to the week ahead.

"What lies behind us and what lies before us are tiny matters compared to what lies within us." ~ Ralph Waldo Emerson

# 1st February
## Camino de Diaz

Cameron Diaz has long been my ultimate woman. Funny, beautiful and you just know she has a good heart. Well of course she does. I know even though I've never met her in real life. I can feel it or I'm crazy. I often joke or should I say state that one day she will be called Cameron Diaz-McKie. A pipe dream I hear you say. Maybe my Cameron has been that person that you wish you could just have one gentle kiss from or walk hand in hand by a river. Maybe she is not a pipe dream and is actually out there. You must believe that your own Cameron or whatever person is out there. That person may be the girl or guy that rides the bus with you when you're heading to the next stop or the person in your exercise class that you think doesn't see you but they do, it's maybe the person sitting across from you in the AA meeting who just gets what you're saying and understand the struggle that you went through because they have also. So, what the hell am I talking about Mrs. Diaz McKie on a blog about the Camino for? One word "love"!

I have always known that it was going to be right up there as one of the subjects I would think about on my walk however it sprang to mind today as that word love had me thinking.

Let me start first by saying some may think I've been lucky in love where I'd say quite the opposite. I've kissed some beautiful women, danced in the arms of great thinkers and laughed with the funniest of girls. I've married then divorced and sailed round the world with love in my mind.

True love. What is that? The reason I'm thinking about this is I awoke this morning to a "Dear John" email from a friend with whom I had had a few dates. A friend I really liked may I add. It wasn't to be and the email was lovely and complimentary however it ended with " I hope you learn to love again one day" that phrase rolled around my brain all day bashing into the soft sides of the dream section then smashing of the reality section before exploding into a million pieces so that each individual piece could perform the same action of asking me "can I learn to love again one day" STOP! I quite literally commanded my thoughts as I knew the answer. It was easy. I don't need to learn to love again. I always have. I know what love at first sight feels like and yes it does happen for non-believers. You learn to live with it in the safe part of you and it can bring you smiles when called upon. So, the question is to me not "will I learn to love again?' but rather "will I be able to love even though part of my heart will always be somewhere else?' Answer I have no idea and that's one of the reasons I believe I'm going on this walk. To understand the enormous brick walls I have built through my lack of dating over the last five years. Why was I so insecure and lonely for all that time? Why did vodka seem like a better friend than anyone and after all that and in preparation for the Camino I feel great and ready to do what I want to do. No loneliness and no fear, just enjoying the present. I don't know what will happen tomorrow. I can dream though and tonight I'll dream that my Cameron is waiting for me as I turn a corner when I'm walking the Camino de Diaz. Dare Greatly I did writing the above trust me.

*"It is not because things are difficult that we do not dare, it is because we do not dare that they are difficult" ~ Seneca*

# 2nd February
## A walk a day helps you walk the way

It's been a busy day however highly enjoyable. I've had notice that my new passport is on its way, all my other items that I ordered are on the way and I have spent time going through my checklist and weighing each item that I'm taking, well what I have so far. This is the crazy part. I was looking at my rather small "pile" of items knowing that I was way below my 9.8kg max that I will take. Then after counting I realised I was at 7.8kg already and I'm still waiting on a few things arriving. That's with me already taking things off the list. I'm so glad I've done this exercise with still 3 weeks to go as I hope that by the end of this week I will have everything and that means trimming things off to get the weight I need. I'm confident I'll get there.

After a trip, I had to make with my pops, I had him drop me off about 8.5miles (13.6km) away from home so I could walk through some of my favourite countryside in Scotland. A place called Loch Eck. It's up and down the hills and I thought it would be another step towards the daily mileage I will be doing. I'm planning on around 15 miles a day however if it's less it's less. I've built in about 5 days for rest or sightseeing or even both to the walk. I know this as I decided to just book my flights home. I was not going to due to thinking what if something happens and I need to quit and the big one of I don't want pressure to get to Santiago. I think the 5 days extra gives me ample time to get there without stressing or even thinking about it. Back in Scotland the 4th April.

As I said before I am also doing a fitness squat challenge on Fatty McFatterson Facebook page and I'm only on day two of the squats and it's hurting my lower back. So, sore foot and lower back the odd time. I maybe always have it however I'm acutely aware of anything just now. Every little bit of pain gets me thinking.

I finished off with my radio show Perpetual Dreams tonight. I volunteer at Dunoon Community Radio 97.4fm on a Tuesday night for my show Perpetual Dreams. It's great fun and it lets me chat about what I'm wanting to do with the walk. All in all, it's been a busy day but enjoyable.

> "The minute you choose to do what you really want to do, it's a different kind of life" ~ Buckminster Fuller

# 3rd February

## Lift your head and look, a whole world is right there

I awoke today and as I stepped out of bed I felt the usual pain in my feet. I've had it for a while now and is always sore in the morning and since I decided I was definitely going to walk the Camino I'm really aware of anything with my feet. Last night knowing what I was to expect in the morning I decided to do the thing you shouldn't do and Google why have I got sore feet in the morning remembering that they are fine once I stretch and move about a bit. I have successfully diagnosed myself with plantar fasciitis as it sounded about right and will go with that as I'm fine when I walk for a bit.

Squat challenge complete I arrived in my kitchen to a mountain of parcels and letters. All very exciting no more than on Christmas Day. Firstly, the important one. My new passport had arrived in just over a week from sending off. Sigh of relief. That was until I opened my new and smooth micro fibre towel. I can't help but wonder how it will dry me however I now understand why it is quick dry. There is not a lot of material. Well what I mean it's not a fluffy bath towel you wrap yourself in and more of a smooth mid-size towel. It is however light and that's what's important. Weight is everything now. New walking underwear arrived and it's very stretchy and I'm looking forward to testing it out. That's weird. Who looks forward to testing their new undies out? Wait, I'll not answer that. Also arriving was a new base t-shirt and my walking poles. They seem fine however it will be strange walking with them but yesterday when coming down a steep hill I thought that they would be handy. Not so excited about testing them as I am the undies. Also, the new shiny relative of the credit card that was out of date by a year arrived today emergency funds.

I then spent the morning preparing and then presenting an hour show on DCR 97.4fm. I really enjoy it and the show I done today is one of 5 I'm recording that will be played when I'm on the Camino. I wonder if any of the places I pass through will have a community radio show. That would be cool to see.

An appointment in the afternoon provided me some time to have a walk around our little town which I don't get a chance to do a lot and I discovered an outdoor clothing shop. Ooft! I was in there all excited and asked the owner when he opened, as I presumed not long ago with all the boxes and new stock, to which he replied oh late 2014!!! I need to keep my eyes open better. It's amazing what you see when you just slow down a bit and look. I learned that when out walking. Keep your head up and look around it's amazing what you see even when you've passed the same spot a thousand times. This was concluded by a 4 mile walk home.

It was art class night. I signed up to a beginner's art class for ten weeks and I have to be honest I really enjoy it. It's so free and fun feeling. I have never done anything like this before so it's all new and interesting. I've decided to take a small sketch pad and one pencil with me. I know every gram is precious but I know there will be small sketches I will want to make. We used ink and bleach in the class tonight which is really fun.

So everything I'm doing seems to always come back to the Camino. Three weeks today I should be in Bayonne. Wow!

*"You gain strength, courage and confidence by every experience in which you really stop to look fear in the face. You must do the thing which you think you can not do" ~ Eleanor Roosevelt*

# 4th February

## There's always time in the day for Yoga

I woke up after a seven-hour straight sleep and it felt great. I had many a night in the past that through worry, alcohol and the always common head racing at a million miles an hour syndrome where sleep was patchy to say the least and came when exhaustion took over. Now I have a problem getting to sleep as I'm busy, busy, busy enjoying life. Today was a good example of busy but in a good way.

When I wake I say hello to the world. Literally say it. Good morning world. I looked on line for current vacancies and updated my CV. I need to figure out what it is I want to do as a career still, a question that has remained unanswered for a long time. After the usual shower I headed downstairs to see what goodies I mean equipment of course had arrived and sure enough there were a pair of shorts, more walking underwear and.... Oh crap I can't remember. I'll need to complete another review of my check list tomorrow.

From a fitness side, today I had a couple of classes. Stretch and tone with my friend/yoga guru Junie in the am and then a yoga class also by Juniein the evening. I get a lot from the yoga class and have a small routine I want to practice daily on the Camino for a couple of reasons. To focus on my breathing, yes I can get lost in that, to keep me subtle and stretched and because I enjoy it in many ways. I just feel good after yoga. I always thought it was a bit deep, you know like let your body sway like a tree in the wind sort of stuff, but it's not been although it has taken me to a different mental level. As in I'm thinking I must be mental to do this. Joking of course.

Between these I ate twice and had a cheeky wee nap on the sofa and before I knew it I was back in the house and it was 9pm. Where did the day go? Radio show tomorrow morning so had to prepare for that also. As I said a good kind of busy.

> *"To many talented people string and unstring their instruments without ever playing their music." ~ Ken Standley*

# 5th February
## Dream flower and reality

I was a bit disappointed today when I arrived in the kitchen to see the spot on the counter normally reserved for a package or two waiting quietly and empty. I nearly went and ordered something as the thought of this was too painful. I liked the daily arrival of some piece of clothing or equipment that is to be my friend over the next so many weeks. This was alleviated when I was leaving to go do my morning radio show and I met the postman who gave me a small but well appreciated package. I opened it in haste as I can't actually remember what I've ordered so it's always a surprise. I sighed when I realised its contents as they were important but "nit" something I was wanting to remember. I wanted to forget all about the potential of bed bugs. Yup it is widely documented that they also do little bed bug pilgrimages and if you're willing they will use you as not only their hostel but also their food supply. I can feel my skin crawling just now however I must be sensible and remember that there are many posts I have read where people have never seen one. However, I bought the stuff they recommend to treat my sleeping bag, ruck sack, bed sheet etc. I figured that it would give me some sort of peace of mind while I'm cocooned in my sleeping bag every night.

I talked a little about the walk on my show then had a shortish walk in the pouring rain. That walk with my daily squat challenge was alas all the exercise I completed however I still feel stronger than I did a month or so ago.

I have a favourite flower which is the sunflower and as I've never painted a flower and always wanted to do a sunflower I sat and relaxed and got my paint brush out and as I painted that flower it patiently listened to a lot of thoughts. It reminds me of reaching out to the sky, beauty, love and overall positivity. The sunflower is a huge symbol of all these things to me. This painting, my first ever of a flower, I called "dream flower" as it knows all my dreams and it knows the person... It's everything that resembles hope.

Tonight, was a bit of a reality check as I had said I am unemployed and the little money I had saved will go to bills over the next month leaving me with the budgeted money I have to walk the Camino. Basically, I'll come back penniless but I could be here in the same situation with not having the experience. That is quite scary shit however I believe that everything will be OK. In fact, not even OK but really good. I just believe. It's good to have the fear but I have to do this. I know that I'm going to learn, make mistakes, learn more. You can't put a price on that. I've decided I'm going to take a notepad and pencil for some sketches.

"If one advances confidently in the direction of his dreams, and endeavours to live the life he has imagined, he will meet with success unexpected in common hours." ~ Henry David Thoreau

# 6th February

## You think and breathe again and start the change

The walk feels even more important than ever now. Three months since I walked out of a hospital with one clear view. To change my life, to be me and honest, to love the good people around me, day by day get a little healthier, a little clearer, love a little better and try and make people smile. Make me smile. Yes, make me smile.

The walk was only a pipe dream as when I came out of hospital I found it hard to walk ten fecking meters never mind do anything else. The focus quite unselfishly, I think, was on myself. I was just happy I was still on this planet. I still am. October 31st was the day I started to change my life, I started to discover me again. Six days in hospital reflecting on life. How I thought I had lived life yet had not even scratched the surface of what real life can be. That's what I'm doing now. I'm scratching away little by little and discovering. I dream of love, adventure and that I can go on to somehow inspire people in a way that will stop them from ever hurting or running away the way I did.

Then there is love. I can only think of one person in my life that I thought I'd fallen in love with, but that is that and I do understand that I have to make an effort, even though I'm shit at it, to be open to the opportunity of love. Who knows the Camino may answer that?

As for preparation for the walk I ate lots. I packed my rucksack for the first time and it felt OK. That was of course only having to walk round the house and my pops and I went to a Burns Supper. That's one person I trust with everything. A great man.

> *"The Journey is what brings us happiness  
> not the destination." ~ Dan Millman*

# 7th February

## Check your gear again in the rain and then poncho it

I slept at most three hours last night so when I woke up at just before nine I didn't want to get out of my bed. That was until I heard the rain on the window. The wind was howling and smashed the rain against my window like someone was throwing a handful of small steel ball-bearings against it every few seconds. It sounded wild and when I looked outside it was nothing short of crazy. My tiredness I knew would wash away with the application of Nivea for Men gel I use every morning in the shower. My goal now was to blow the cobwebs away from my previous night's thoughts and head out into this storm to walk and test my waterproofs to the max.

Another product I had bought was a set of 3 clear waterproof document carriers. The small one I thought would do for my phone and found that I could still seal it so that my headphones came out and it was pretty much watertight. It was going to have to be. To my amazement, the touch pad still worked through the plastic which is really handy. I also used the leather waterproof stuff "Dubbins" on my boots as it was so wet. I had been trying to keep them in good health. Off I set with an amazon love songs playlist in my ears and thoughts of the Camino on my mind. The rain and wind were violent to say the least however I found that walking in it was invigorating. I had my favourite blue cap on with the word love on it. I love that cap. I walked for about five miles and met up with my pops for lunch. This is when I discovered that my waterproof jacket was not so waterproof, the softshell jacket was not so either and the deliberate navy-blue cotton t-shirt I had as a base layer showed up nicely the wet areas. Everywhere bar where my day pack sat on my back. This was not good as during a normal bout of rain a few days ago everything was fine but now with heavy rain it was not. Action would have to be taken so I'm going to order a poncho. That seems to be recommended and will decide if I take the waterproof jacket now. My legs were fine in the waterproof trousers and my feet were as dry as a bone.

I retreated to my bed in the afternoon as I was tired and slept for a bit before spending time looking at ponchos on the Internet. I had to stop myself and say, "Iain it's a ponchono need to spend hours here." Oh, I nearly forgot. I tried my new Under Armour underwear today. It was good. A bit itchy at first as its new so that didn't look too great as I walked down the road scratching for the first half mile. All was just fine and comfy after.

I did wave at two cars today by mistake while walking. That always amuses me as for an instant you and said driver, who both waved back, are saying who was that. I think I'll wave at more people. Deliver a bit of happiness to the world.

*"The only obligation in any lifetime is to be true to yourself." ~ Richard Bach*

# 8th February
## Who would I like to walk with

It's just after 4am and I didn't update this last night as I was, for some reason, exhausted so when I toddled off to bed I must have been asleep within seconds. The day in preparation terms for the Camino was a walk which was nice as for once it was not raining. A poncho and earplugs were also ordered and I need to look at what type of charger/adaptor I'll take for my phone. The one piece of electrical/communication equipment I will take as it covers emergency call, photo, blog update, music etc. As I lay in the dark I also got thinking about arriving in Bayonne. I had an email to say that the cheap hotel I booked reception closes at 7pm and as my flight does not land till five thirty pm I need to figure out what it is they are trying to say about an access code in their email. Q the French language lesson/help from someone. I don't know why I'm so nervous about the arrival in France. I managed to get around Paris OK when I was there but I think I'll be more relaxed when I get to the starting town of SJDP.

Another thought I had when lying in bed was if I had to choose a different person each day to walk with then who would that be. It could be anyone from history or present. So, if I was going to say it would take 33 days then I have to choose 33 people. I'm going to make this list over the next few days. Who would it be and why? I like this idea.

> "Optimism is the one quality more associated with success and happiness than any other." ~ Brian Tracy

# 9th February
## Just these words

"Your time is limited, so don't waste it living someone else's life. Don't be trapped by dogma —which is living with the results of other people's thinking. Don't let the noise of other's opinions drown out your own inner voice. And most important, have the courage to follow your heart and intuition. They somehow already know what you truly want. Everything else is secondary." ~ Steve Jobs (1955 — 2011)

# 10th February

## And yes, there is fear

I have now not walked for the last couple of days. No excuse really. I have spent a lot of time doing things for the radio show as I have 2 extra shows this week and I helped a couple of the girls who have a show today. So, by the time I finished that then went for a sandwich with pops, had a fifteen-minute nap and then went to my art class it was after nine pm. Victor who runs the radio station has asked me to go in and talk about the trip on an hour interview next week. That should be interesting as I'm still trying to figure out myself what heck I'm doing.

I did receive my poncho today that I tried on. It's OK and bright orange. I said to pops it was in case I get lost. I really hope I don't get lost. I don't know why my mind keeps saying follow the yellow brick road, follow the yellow brick road.

So, it's two weeks today and I'll be in France. I am getting a bit nervous, a bit of fear about not training the way I said I would, sleeping in that mummy sleeping bag, my feet not holding up, leaving pops, not having enough cash to pay bills etc. However, I'm glad I have all these fears and a few more. I'd be more worried if I didn't. I just think to myself that I'm the man in the arena and then a wave of excitement literally flows through my body. Tomorrow is Yoga day though so still doing important things.

> *"Courage doesn't mean you don't get afraid. Courage means you don't let fear stop you." ~ Bethany Hamilton*

# 12th February

## Day dreams of the people list

Less than two weeks to go. The countdown is on and I fear I may be thinking too much unconsciously as I seem to have been a bit sensitive to stuff today. Nothing that I should have been about however my mind is kind of taking in a million things that I keep thinking I need to do then not doing anything as I know I have pretty much done most things and got the things I need.

My walking hat arrived so that was exciting as I like it and the ear plugs arrived also. Seemingly these are good things to have as people can snore a lot in the places you stay. I'm told I snore a little but I don't believe it as I sleep on my front. I tried these silicon ear plugs and I reckon I'll need to get back up foam ones just in case.

Fitness wise I attended a stretch and tone class then went for a good walk then a yoga class tonight and day 11 of the squat challenge we are doing. My legs were a bit achy tonight and I thought that I love a bath when I have a couple of legs that ache. Makes me think if I'll somehow be able to treat myself to a bath along the way.

I also had to send an email to the hotel in Bayonne I'm staying as they don't have anyone on reception after 7pm and there is a good chance I'll arrive after that. I just remembered I need to figure out how to get there from the airport. I received an email to tell me my room and a code to get in. I don't know where the code is for. If it's a room or outside door. No idea but I'll find out when I arrive.

I also played with watercolour painting that I started for the first-time last night. I tried a sunset and I think it looked more like a primary school attempt but it has potential when I figure out colour and generally watercolours. It's fun though so I will now take a small sketch pad and a couple of pencils, a sharpener and rubber to have a go at sketching when I'm there. Well that's the plan.

I also had a think about the thirty-three people I would like to walk with for a day. Some are not alive but the thought is good to imagine walking with them. The people who are alive you never know. These are the people I have so far and part or all the reason. I'll have the whole list and reasons by the time I leave. I do know who I'd like to (on the imaginary walk with one of these people a day walk) be on the first day and who would be the last day and the reasons why. So, in no particular order here are the people so far and a couple of words towards why.

Gandhi his amazing mind, courage and strength
Donna F — Let her see who the real me is and we can laugh
Billy Connolly, funny and interesting. Tell a few stories
Junie Jones, Yoga guru who inspires
Bill Bailey so clever and funny.
Michael Palin — I loved his round the world books plus
the Life of Brian is the funniest movie I've ever seen
Amanda R positive, funny and friend
Jimmy Carr he'd make me laugh with his energy
Stephen Fry clever funny guy
Einstein don't know what I'd ask but it would be great
to see what he thought about today's world
God I have no doubt I'll try to understand more as I walk
An Alien there has to be friendly ones. Just talk about normal things
Paulo Calieo talk about his life
Pops would just be great to share part of it with him
Mum I know she will be there all the way
Cameron(son) one day I hope. Walk and talk
about everything he has done in life.
Sister we would have fun and just talk
Tom Hanks an amazing actor and my favorite movie is Forrest Gump
Cameron Diaz she's beautiful and funny. Who wouldn't
want to have a day walking with her
Richard Branson the guy just is inspiring when he talks. Have a day
just talking about how to make the world a better place for everyone.

I'm sure more will come to me and why.

"You must be the change you wish to see in the world." ~ Mahatma Gandhi

# 13th February

## Blisters and new beginnings

Another walk today that was only around four miles however my right foot still is giving me issues and can be sore. Still think it's that planter something as I said before I googled it and stopped short of the self-amputation advice that was inevitably going to come. The unthinkable also happened and when I arrived home I was feeling a couple of what I may describe as hotspots on the balls of my feet. WHAT?!!! signs of the start of blisters after 4 miles and just a few days in a row walking. I was laughing to myself thinking I have to do about fifteen miles a day for a month and I get hotspots after a few miles a few days in a row. I checked my first aid kit to make sure the Compeed and other blister relief was there. On reading the info I had on blister prevention and treatment and to no comfort I remembered the statement I read in a guide about the "inevitable blisters" everyone gets. From a prevention point of view, I have bought the correct socks, good fitting boots, learned a better way to lace said boots etc. Only thing is I didn't wear those socks, tie the laces the way they should to prevent slipping or "it puts the lotion on the skin" stuff to make the skin better. Note to self. Do what the experts advise to do every time you walk.

The above however really did not worry me as I had woken up to one message today. It's funny when I smoked I'd wake up and through bleary eyes instinctively spark up a cig and inhale the blue smoke into my lungs waiting for that kick that would neither wake me up nor make me feel better. Now I have another habit. I wake up and through bleary eyes check my social media outlets and sometimes I do get a kick if you get a message. I had just one this morning and it made me smile. It made me think about the inevitable step away from constant social media, that has taken over so many of our lives at times, when I'm on my walk. I don't down it, in fact I embrace it in many ways but I know that it will no longer be the partner I wake up next to every day. That is good I believe. I do have to write a blog every day though.

While walking today and thinking about when the odd person asks me why I'm doing this I find it extremely hard to put into words. I call it my Camino Dream and I can feel and understand that in myself but it's hard to explain. It's like a lifetime of things all coming to a point. Where do you start? A volume of books that each would have their own joy or tragedy within the story they hold. All with a common theme that's me. All crossing over in subtle and some not so subtle ways in their race to pull me to this one point. The starting point! Is it a new starting point? I don't know I just know I have to do it. To open a new volume and let life, my life, start writing another story.

"To accomplish great things, we must not only act, but also dream; not only plan, but also believe." ~ Anatole France

# 14th February
## What book to read

A lovely walk today that tested my waterproof jacket again. It was slightly different as it was sleet and wind that was the test and the clothing stood up to the test pretty good. After deciding yesterday to make sure I wear the correct socks and lace the boots properly I went walking in the clothes I will walk the Camino in. While it was pouring down its rain and sleet I felt warm and that gave me a good feeling however I hope I don't get to many days of sleet in Spain. If so I'll be prepared. The way I laced my boots make huge difference also.

Other than the walk not much else regarding the walk happened other than I put in a packet of those plastic floss/toothpick things that look like a shark fin. I use them all the time so while they are a few grams they are necessary to me.

I remembered thinking today that I usually walk listening to music that I'll probably not want to listen the whole time when on the Camino however I will have to ensure I have the correct playlists for the times I do want and I'll need to download a book on my phone just in case I feel the need to read. I don't know what one though as usually I only read things that are recommended to me. I find that fun and interesting. The other part of the day was eating a beautiful pizza with pops and a friend. Purely training food of course then I practised a bit more of my new found past time art. Today I painted a thistle.

*"The future belongs to those who believe in the beauty of their dreams." ~ Eleanor Roosevelt*

# 15th February

## The surprises to come

It's been a couple of beautiful days to be walking, which I have done, and thinking of what is to come. I had looked through a Camino Twitter site briefly last night and some of the pictures which surprised me with urban areas and paths littered with pilgrims that resembled the last stage of a local 10k run. Lots of colours and people just strolling. My mind has this image of no one else around and mile after mile of countryside. There are some pretty big towns along the way and lots of villages from what I've read and seen on the map however I've kind of deliberately stayed away from too many pictures as I'm looking forward to the newness and first time seeing it all. Kind of why I only ever read a short bit of Paulo's book The Pilgrimage. I didn't want to have my thoughts taken away with something. I want it to be lots of surprises. I hope. I have not studied the route to be honest as I thought I will look at the next day the day before in the guide book. I know it's thirty-three stages, or more if I rest or walk less, and I know what day one looks like and I dream of the last day completion but I have no idea what that will be like.

Anyway, the walks were good and I purchased some euros so

I have a little cash for the first few nights then I'll take it from there. I still need to spray my cover sheet and rucksack etc. with the bedbug stuff. I'll try not to think about those wee things and I really need to try walking some sort of distance with my rucksack to see how it feels. Not before I re-check all the gear I have and the list. Oh, and this may sound disgusting and it is a bit bogging in a way but I wore my quick drying underpants and top as well as my 1000-mile socks for a couple of days to experiment with how they handled I still showered and all was OK. They didn't completely stink. Which reminds me that one bit of advice I read was sleep in the clothes you're walking in the next day then when you get up don't shower just walk and shower at night. I think I'll find that hard as I can't function in the morning without a shower however they say that you get used to it.

Well tomorrow night I go on the local radio to chat about this for an hour and I don't really know what to say but I'm sure it will be fine and it still doesn't feel like I'm going to do this.

> *"Those who dance are considered insane by those who can't hear the music." ~ George Carlin*

# <u>16th February</u>

Interview on DCR 97.4FM

As far as training or organising goes there was nothing done today. I spent the morning painting a highland coo and the afternoon preparing for my radio show. I did however go on Victors show to talk about the Camino and it's the most I've probably talked about it. It's funny as I know in myself why I'm doing it and what it's for and I tried to explain that the best I could. It was fun talking about the walk though. This is the address of where to listen to it.

https://www.mixcloud.com/iain-mckie2/why-the-camino-de-santiago-iains-interview-on-victor-and-carols-show

The only other things I completed in preparation was eating too much food. My theory is that you can carry around ten percent so if I put on a few kilos I can take more stuff. Joke of course. I also decided to buy a small Swiss Army knife. It has a nail file, scissors and small knife on it. The thought behind is file for any jaggy bits on nails of course, scissors in case of things such as bandage cutting, nail trimming, making paper snowflakes and the knife for using with pack lunch or anything else. It's only a few grams but may come in handy.

I have a busy few days ahead with radio and yoga so have to fit Camino stuff in. Not that I have much to do. Walk a bit with my rucksack, spray my sheet etc. It will be here before I know it.

*"I am an artist at living, my work of art is my life." ~ D.T. Suzuk*

# 17th February
## Take risks and face your fears

A week today I fly out to France and it does not feel like it. I know while I have walked a lot it's not anywhere near the amount I should have done. I keep thinking of the blog where a pilgrim said that you do a lot of your fitness training on the Camino. That's my excuse.

A weird thing happened last night when I woke up and felt really homesick even though I was in my own bed. I don't know if I had been dreaming but the realisation of being away for 6 weeks felt quite real and very long. My mind was racing with fear of what if I hate this, what if I don't see anyone and I'm just plodding along, what happens if my feet stay sore and I can't do it. I had to take control of my mind that was racing away with what are quite legitimate questions and think about it's probably not enough time to see everything, there are going to be amazing people and sit down if your feet are sore. I think it must be normal when you're doing something to have a lot of different thoughts racing through your head although at times I go ages without thinking about it.

My sister bought this as a large poster at Christmas for me. I had it framed and it hangs in my bedroom. I love the message and it was one of many things that helped me make my decision to do the Camino.

"You only get one life. Do what makes you happy, and spend time with those who make you smile. If you're not happy, do something about it. If your friends don't have time for you, find new ones. If you want something go and get it, what's stopping you? Life is short, don't wonder what if, you don't know if you don't try. Always follow your heart. Have no regrets. Some opportunities only come once, seize them. Don't dwell on your past mistakes. Accept the things in life you can't change. Try not to care what other people think of you. Don't compare the gains or fortunes of others with yours. Always give 100% in everything you do. Have dreams and aspirations. Love and be loved. Stop over analysing. Surround yourself with ones you love and things you enjoy doing. Smile at others and laugh as much as you can. Forgive quickly, embrace change, travel often. Don't be afraid to fail. Try new things. Take Risks. Face your fears. Decide what you want to do in life and go for it. Don't wait for things to happen, make them happen. Life is one big adventure, you only get one, so make it as good and happy as possible."

# 18th February

## Let the checks begin

Waking up at 6am this morning I felt strangely pleased as I was thinking I need to be getting into a habit of getting up sharp when I'm on the Camino so that I'm not too far away from first light when I head off. The reason being I figured if I walk around 6 hours a day then if I'm away early it gives me lots of time to take in sights, places of interest or take a rest and be at the place I'm staying in daylight where it gives me time to have a look around, get a shower, do my washing and eat. This however may change when I get there so who knows. As far as places of interest and due to my quite deliberate not looking at possible places of interest I find it exciting what each day may bring.

I also was thinking about food today and I've read about the wide range of options I will have in either cooking for myself or buying the pilgrims menu which is a three-course dinner every night for around €10. I decided very quickly I can't see me cooking unless my budget takes a hit somehow. I'm not a huge fish fan however I think it may be an essential "just try it" as it does have a lot of great nutrients I'm told. Oh, that reminds me of the funniest jokes I've heard in a while.

What was the last thing a fish said after he had been run over by a bus -----Oh McGill's! you have to be from around these parts to get that and if you're not then McGills is the name of a bus company.

Equipment wise I bought the last piece today in the form of a fitted single sheet. As the hostels/refugios/albergues I'm staying in do have the possibility of bed bugs it's advised to take one and I also treated it and my rucksack etc in Permethrin. The anti-bed bug stuff that is meant to work. However, after about five minutes of reading blogs on bed bugs there were so many different views and old wife's tales I thought I'll do this and then see what happens. No point in worrying about what may not happen in that department.

Today was also the last day of my yoga classes. Not my last day of yoga as Junie my amazing yoga teacher has given me the practice I need to be doing daily when I'm away however I won't see the ladies and gents from the class for seven weeks. Yoga has been such a great thing for me personally and I feel I get great benefit from it both mentally and physically. It will be an important part of my daily routine.

Back to the equipment. I believe I have everything now and I have again laid it all out. I'll check it again tomorrow and weigh it all piece by piece again. As I'm only meant to carry 10% of my body weight that means 9.8kg and I know that I'm over that so need to look at what I can cut out once more. I did make an excuse to friends that the reason I'm stuffing my face all the time lately was so I would carry more.

> "So many of our dreams at first seem impossible, then they seem improbable and then, when we summon the will, they soon become inevitable." ~ Christopher Reeve

# 19th February

Note to self – Do not watch the movie Hostel 3 again before I go

This morning I arrived in the kitchen after a night of around five good hours of sleep and ready to head off to the radio station for an extra show. I then had a few things to do today in regard to checking and double checking a few things.

The first thing I saw was the local paper, the Dunoon Observer, who had written a nice article about the walk. I must thank Chris Martin for his great words about my journey. Heading to the local radio station I presented my show and after I had an hour to get the Camino haircut. I usually have my very thinning hair cut every two to three weeks so it was cut today and that will be it till the end of the Camino unless something happens along the way where I decide to go all Britney Spears.

I then met pops, Junie, her mum and her partner Richard for lunch and a chat about the walk. People I've spoken with seem to be genuinely interested in what it is and why I'm doing it. I felt some great energy off them. It was funny as before I met them I had went into a shop or two looking for a Scotland patch that I wanted to put on my rucksack to be told that nowhere does them. I don't believe that in the whole of Dunoon there is not a Scotland patch? Probably not a bad thing as I'm not great at sewing. However, Junie's mum had bought me a little Scotland pin which I was really surprised and thankful for. No sewing now required and said pin is proudly on my rucksack. Heading home from lunch with pops and Junie we managed to acquire fudge doughnuts. Yum. So, I'm now in the middle of the afternoon realising that I was also going out for dinner so my attempt to watch my diet had again been blown for the day.

With a couple of hours to spare before dinner I was going to weigh all my equipment when my friend said stick a movie on and chill out. That was great until I sat and watched an hour and thirty minutes of the Hostel 3. Great movie choice a few days before I head off to stay in hostels for over a month. Deep breathes and equipment weigh in postponed till Saturday.

After a lovely dinner with my dad at new local place I lay on the couch looking up info for the walk. Things I was again trying to find out was how do I get from the airport to the hotel on the first night. I have found this an adventure in itself as my French is "merde' so after many different web pages and out of date blogs I have postponed that also until Saturday. Second time that's been postponed however I'm sure it will work out. My other check was that I had read that I can pick up my Camino Passport the credentials you take that lets you stay in the refugios and get stamped to prove you walked the Camino at the town I set off from. I then read that the pilgrims office only opens in season and had to try and re check that. I found their website that said they were open all year however that was two years ago. I'll find out when I get there I guess. If not, I can pick a passport up on the second day I believe. I need to not worry about these things as it's all part of the journey.

In all, great eating all day and probably the only practical thing I completed was I checked in for my flights and printed the boarding passes. In honesty, it's all pretty much done so no point in making things up to do so enjoying time with family and friends.

*"Fortune favours the brave." ~ Terence*

# 20th February

Buen Camino — who will I say that to first

Buen Camino which literally means "good path" is the phrase used by pilgrims when they meet each other and is a way of saying good luck and happy travelling. I also read this which I like "It is an acknowledgement that you see a person who is searching for "perfection". This is related to the "pilgrimage" intent. Becoming your best self is the goal."

I heard Buen Camino while watching the movie "The Way" tonight and it made me think about who would be the first person/pilgrim I'd say this to and who would be the first person to say it to me when I'm there. The thought did give me a rush of excitement and a sudden explosion of what will this or that be like detonated in my mind.

I had decided to watch the movie again as I couldn't really remember it from the first time I watched it. In fact, I couldn't even say when it was I seen it other than in the last six or seven months (and as I typed that I remembered). It was the girl in the bar who had done the Camino and I must have watched it while travelling up the north of Scotland. So yes, about seven months ago. Mmmm a lot of changes since then. It's funny watching the movie this time as I'm recognising a lot of the things they are talking about. I am laying in my bed watching it thinking I'm going there in a few days! It was a bit of an emotional deep breath moment if I'm honest. Exciting though. The movie is on pause as I write this in case I drift off to my Camino Dream. It is a good movie that's well worth a watch. Another thing that makes me think. I go to sleep with the TV on every night and it switches itself off. Well seeing I'm single. Not having TV and the having to sleep in the mummy sleeping bag is definitely a test that's coming up.

I postponed, again, the weighing of equipment as it won't take long. I have added something new that's not essential however I will over the next few days decide. It's a new small set of watercolour paints. I have an idea of taking about forty-one little 3" by 4" bits of watercolour paper and doing a tiny watercolour of something every day. I've only started painting just over a week ago but I love it. It's new, exciting and rewarding. I already have a sketch pad and two pencils in my pack. Maybe I should just get an easel and a life model instead of the pack and do a painting trip. Seriously though I will need to be a bit ruthless on what extras I take.

I have also solved a problem. I was up to nineteen people who I'd like to walk a day of the Camino with -imaginary/dream from a previous day.   The issue I was having was I couldn't think of others either because I was too busy eating or doing paintings that I thought that what I'd do was ask each of the nineteen people on my imaginary walk to nominate one person to spend a day with me. I wonder who Richard Branson would send on the walk with me or Gandhi. Would Billy Connolly send a comedian or a well-versed historian? It's a nice imagine wondering who. The extra days I'd spend it with that one person and talk about life and freeness while laughing till we reached the end of the Camino. We're all allowed that dream.

Training? Today was another busy day of a certain type of training. Time with pops and friends with lots of good food. It started off with a most important training principle. The foot massage and scrub. I have to admit I now get why people go and get pampered. I enjoyed it and have promised myself to get a bit of pampering more often. Then it was off for some amazing food again with pops. Tonight was an easy night of chilling out, organising some credit card stuff and paying some bills before meeting with some friends for an hour or two. I shall now watch the end of The Way. Maybe tomorrow I'll weigh my equipment! Then again who knows.

*"Dance for yourself, if someone understands, good. If not then no matter, go right on doing what you love." ~ Lois Hurst*

# 21st February

## Packing done — until tomorrow when it may change

I woke up with the thought of no longer postponing the weighing of my equipment. Then my friend called to go for coffee so the weigh in was postponed till after morning coffee. The weighing of equipment was fine as I had already done it a while back so it was a double check and add on any new equipment. I weighed every single piece separately and when totalled up it came to 10.2kg. As my suggested limit was 9.91kg I thought that this was pretty spot on. I was happy as this included my sketch pad, two pencils and a small set of watercolour paints. I'm wanting to do that small painting a day thing so they are in.

Pleased with the weigh in I had a second weigh in which was more of a how much of this food training has added to my overall weight. It has a pound or so. I also measured my neck 16.5", waist 43"? I think I must be measuring it wrong but that was the smallest bit. My weight was 218.6 lbs. the Camino is not about losing weight however the reason I took these measurements was I'll be interested in the effect on my body it has.

After the shock of the weigh in I took inspiration from my alltime favourite movie Forrest Gump. Why the Camino Iain I just feel like walking is my Gump inspired answer.

I completed my "I'm travelling" banking arrangements and have now deleted all of my phone apps that I won't need to allow me enough memory for photos. I have kept a handful of photos on my phone. A couple of my family. Pops, mum, my sis and her wee ones, one of my son, a couple friends and a couple of inspirational quotes that I love.

Tonight I packed my rucksack. I've never packed anything more than a day before I leave for anywhere before. This is an amazing feat that I have completed. The sleeping bag takes up most of the room as it's a four season one so it is thicker. The rest I have put in a way I think of what I may need is easily accessible e.g. waterproof things at the top. I tried it on with it full and I have to admit I can feel the weight so it may take some getting used to and adjusting. I'll unpack and pack a couple of times again before I go to see if I can try different ways.

> *"Success is not final, failure is not fatal: it is the courage to continue that counts." ~ Winston Churchill*

# 22nd February

## Have fun every day

During the night my stomach was rumbling and I was feeling a bit dodgy to say the least. I was thinking to myself if you're going to be sick do it now and get it over with but after an eventual few hours of rest I was fine and ready to continue my training in the eating department. You'd think I was never going to eat properly again the way I'm going. Note to selfSpain has nice food. Maybe it's my body subconsciously stocking up as it knows it's going to do a lot of exercise.

This morning was an important and wonderful time that was both powerful and emotional. I had asked the Reverend Joseph Stewart if he would come say a prayer and a blessing for my walk. I had read that no matter what religion you were that this was a good thing to do if you so desired and I did desire. While I'm not insanely religious I do believe something and this was important to me. When the Rev Joe arrived, I was outside making a video to promote my radio show that I present. All as a bit of fun and the Rev Joe is great and just laughed and my antics. Pops and I chatted with him for a while and then we stood and he placed both his hand and my dad's hand on my head and gave me the most beautiful and meaningful blessing and prayer. That was an emotional and powerful moment. I thank you Rev Joe.

It was then off to purchase some duct tape, visit the bank and of course the inevitable head out to eat lunch. When I arrived back home I was pretty tired so slept for a couple of hours in the afternoon and then painted a couple of things at night as I enjoy the relaxation of doing that. Pre-walk relaxation I'm calling it as it still feels a bit like this is not happening then I'll get the odd sudden burst of excitement. I may re pack my kit tomorrow although I don't know why I would. I think I'm just trying to make something up to do. Or maybe I'll just go for lunch.

*"Taking time to do nothing often brings every-thing into perspective." ~ Doe Zantamata*

# 23rd February
## Twas the night before

The funny part of today was that it was beautiful and sunny and I had to visit my friend Jill who lives a mere twenty-minute walk away however I decided I didn't want to walk so jumped on a bus. I figured I'd be doing a lot of walking so just relax. Even though I have done little walking today I have somehow managed to get a stinging hotspot on top of one of my toes. Ha-ha how can that happen. I hardly walked and start to get the start of a blister!!! I said to pops that I couldn't believe it. Compeed may be getting used sooner than I thought. These two things amused me.

This morning was the first time I have woken and thought WOW. I'm away tomorrow and it must be on my mind more than I thought as I did get a wee bit emotional a couple of times today saying see you later to folks and when thinking about things. I also was questioning myself about exactly why was I doing this and then getting excited. A day of emotions indeed. I kept my mind busy with painting and the radio show tonight. I will miss doing the radio and look forward to that when I return.

Mostly everything is done and I will double check my pack

after I write this. I'm still not believing I'm going to be doing this so will paint something and listen to some music. I fear I may not sleep tonight even though I'm tired. I will however think about the lovely messages I have had from people. The positivity and kind words really do touch me and I know my mind will ponder them and that I'll look at them as I travel.

So, my Camino Dream in becoming more real by the hour. I don't know what is to come but I know I'll embrace it all with every step and breath. I'll think of life and love and try and deliver some happiness along the way. A burst of excitement again as a few tears of emotion, I have no idea where they have come from, dance down my cheek. Wow this is happening. I am excited! This is my Dream!

*"And the day came when the risk to remain tight in a bud was more painful than the risk it took to blossom." ~ Anais Nin*

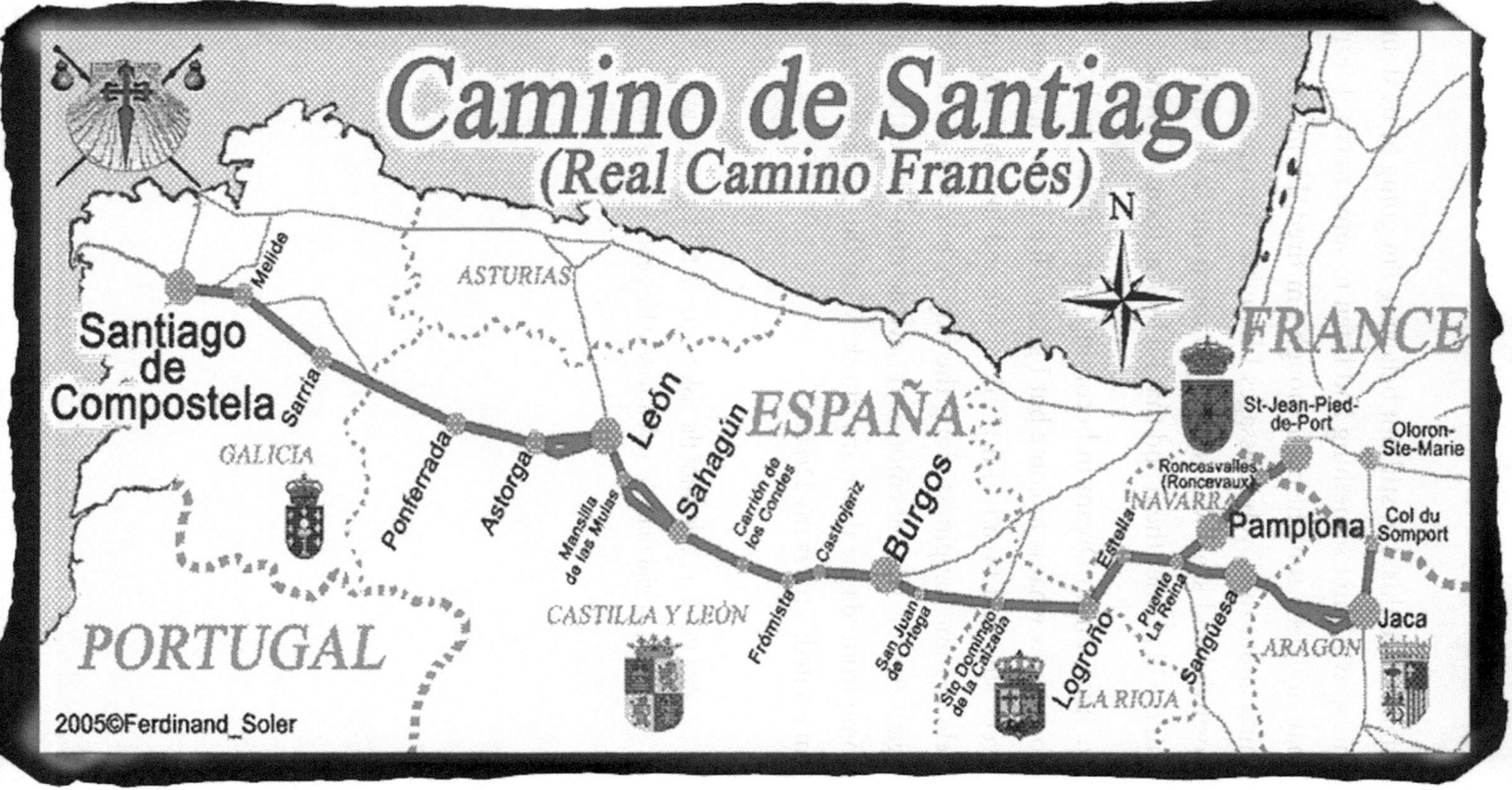
Camino de Santiago
(Real Camino Francés)
N
FRANCE
ESPAÑA
PORTUGAL
ASTURIAS
GALICIA
CASTILLA Y LEÓN
NAVARRA
LA RIOJA
ARAGON
Santiago de Compostela
Melide
Sarria
Ponferrada
Astorga
León
Mansilla de las Mulas
Sahagún
Carrión de los Condes
Frómista
Castrojeriz
Burgos
San Juan de Ortega
Sto Domingo de la Calzada
Logroño
Estella
Puente La Reina
Sangüesa
Pamplona
Roncesvalles (Roncevaux)
St-Jean-Pied-de-Port
Oloron-Ste-Marie
Col du Somport
Jaca
2005©Ferdinand_Soler

## Chapter 2 – My journey on the Camino

# 24th February

Bonjour France
Bayonne

I have arrived in Bayonne I am buzzing.

A quite distinct lack of sleep last night that I thought may happen. I slept for about three hours and woke up just before four am with the thought of I really want a sausage and egg McMuffin.

I lay in bed and tried to feel the comfiness of it and give each of my pillows a hug knowing that it may be some time before I have six pillows again. In fact, even one. Eventually deciding to just get up and shower I thought that we could catch the even earlier ferry. I have turned into my dad and now embrace getting there early to anything or leaving early to get somewhere. No stress and you just toddle along which also gives you time to stop for the aforementioned sausage and egg McMuffin times two. The breakfast of champions is my excuse today.

Glasgow airport was fine and after giving pops a hug and saying see you in 6 weeks I set off through security with my scallop shell proudly dancing on my chest. It's not the normal "bling" one would wear.

Airports are great places. The people excited to be going on holiday, getting the drinks in because that's what you do in Glasgow at 9am that's just the staff! Business travellers topping up on coffee while others parade up and down talking loudly enough on their phone that you can hear them mention business type lingo. Probably on their first or very rare business trip somewhere and feeling all excited and they feel the need to let the people around know what they're up to. They will fling out words like spreadsheet and conference call while explaining to the listener how wonderful their current project is. There really is no need to do it and have a "look at me attitude". Ah wait I am walking about with a big scallop shell attached to my chest that screams look at me!!!! But that's different is it not?

Also on the way in it felt good that I didn't smoke any more. Nearly 100 days ago I just said no more and that was that. Not bad after thirty a day. I used to be with those smoker McSmokersons getting seventeen cigs in before I had to go through security while wondering, if I needed to, could I get back outside if I "really needed one". No more and it is indeed a more relaxing experience and good feeling at the airport. I strode by with my rucksack on as if I was Mr Fitness and had never done an unhealthy thing in my life. Ha-ha I think that can be quite disputed.

London was fine and I had never been in Stanstead before. The queue to go through security was really busy so I just stood and people watched. Some older couple were told to go in one line and another old guy about five places behind decided that the couple had "jumped" the queue. The following word exchange was well worth ignoring. Why? as I was on my way.

Another quick flight, which I slept most off, saw us touch down in Biarritz, France. A small airport and I had been nervous at home about getting to the hotel in the town of Bayonne which is about 8km away. It was easy. Outside and onto the #14 bus which I just said Bayonne Train station in my newly acquired French lingo and with an exchange of €1 I was trundling along on my first ever French public transport bus. It was exciting as well as interesting looking at the different types of houses. It's a big place and all I could figure out from the map was get off the bus near the river. For such a big place everyone seemed really polite to the driver and even though they would get off in the middle of the bus they would all shout thank you and goodbye down the bus. I felt that I should do this also so when I spotted the river I dinged the bell and with a spring in my step a shouted "Merci au revoir" the bus driver replied "see you later mate" joking of course.

With my map reading skills, I knew where I was and I headed to the hotel in the centre of town. It is down a beautiful little street that has cafes down either side and when I went in it was rather incredible. Two stars of sheer eloquence. The room has pillows which is great and one of those French windows with a balcony that you can't go out on but feel you could reach across and touch the apartments on the other side of the street.

Immediately I felt the urge to explore and went for a walk around the old town of Bayonne. It was beautiful in the dusk light and I walked along the river passing the many restaurants and bars where the locals were drinking wine and beer in the cool evening talking about who was the guy with the huge scallop shell walking about. I still haven't taken it off.

It was time to eat and a pizza was in my mind. Simply because I had no clue what all the things were on the menus as I read in passing. Pizza is the same so I sat outside the Pizzeria and realised other than tomato and onion I had no idea what the toppings were. The owner and pizza man did not speak too much English so I put my French skills into action. I pointed at one, said merci and then said café. With smiles and laughter my mystery pizza was ordered and the We-Fe code not pronounced Wi-Fi was delivered.

My Tuna pizza arrived with an espresso coffee. So that's what that word meant tuna. This was a first so when in Rome or Bayonne to be precise I tucked into my first ever tuna pizza washed down with strong coffee. It was delicious. I think though that's because I'm all excited they could have put anything down and I would have eaten it.

Day one so far so good. It's a beautiful place and I'll walk some more now as it's dark and the lights along the river are just beautiful.

*"Walk with your head held up, there's a whole world you're missing if you don't." ~ moi*

# 25th February
## Starting place
## St. Jean Pied de Port

I awoke after a well needed rest and slept more hours than normal so was awake around 7am local time. Perfect I thought as I will now be on the time I want to wake up from now on.

My room had a shared toilet and shower for the whole floor so I headed down to indulge myself in said shower. It was great and I was thinking I hope the rest of the showers ahead of me are just as good. Feeling refreshed I headed for breakfast which is set in the most what I'd call French looking dining room. The breakfast was continental and I had two bowls. One with the biggest amount of cornflakes and a small empty one. Which do I use I thought! I opted for putting some in the small bowl and enjoyed these washed down with coffee and croissant. While enjoying my very French breakfast in the very French dining room the very French hotel dog came for a visit. I say very French as it was wearing a beret! Joke obviously. It was the onions around its neck! Anyway, as I was about to say hello I quickly thought wait it's a French dog so won't understand that. Say bonjour. I did and it trotted on over speaking dog that I could swear was eeeeoh eeeeoh. Petting my new French buddy I was asking his name over and over. The dog stopped and looked at me. "Quelle heure est-il, Quelle heure est-il" I continued to ask him. I have now discovered I was asking the dog the time. I finished breakfast with him and we both enjoyed it as he sat in his obviously well-trained give me some food please position.

Heading the short distance across town I found the train station no problem. Using my new found French speaking skills I ordered a ticket to the starting point of my walk St Jean Pied De Port. The woman was obviously impressed with not only my language skills but the actual French accent that seemed to automatically go with them. She even laughed. I suspect from happiness and not at my French accent. Ticket purchased I waited in the station and looked out the huge glass doors at the rain beating down. This did not bother me at all. One thing did slightly bother me. There were five rucksacks in the train station and 4 people. One person with hiking boots and was outside. This person I assumed was the owner of the unattended rucksack. Said person I thought was on the phone however every time the large automatic doors opened I could hear him singing and noticed he was dancing to. I thought great I'm walking the Camino with Rain Man. I called him that not after the movie but the fact that it was pissing down with rain.

I continued to wait on the train and was quite happy just waiting. It's amazing when you're not in a rush to get somewhere you can just watch the world for a while and it's quite relaxing.

On the train, I met Xavier Mr Singing and Dancing who said to me that he was happy that he was not the only one who's lost it. I reflected on the aforementioned singing which he told me was to energise him as he was tired. I shall now try this. He is from Columbia now living in the Netherlands. Xavier said to me I think I have a lot of things in my pack. He said I have a sleeping bag. Ah OK I said. then a pause. Then he said I have a tent also, ah OK I said, then a pause, he looked over to me and he says I have a swimming pool to, I laughed then and so did he, another pause and he said I have a mini bar too. I burst out laughing. I like this friendly singing joking guy from Columbia who lives in Holland I thought.

I also met Britt a young lady from Canada and Eduardo from Italy. Our train journey was spent chatting and laughing and even how we could set up a business hiring out donkeys or if we should hire a donkey. The countryside that was whizzing by reminded me of Scotland. Green, rivers and rain. The houses were different but apart from that I could be on the 8.45am from Gourock to Glasgow. But I wasn't. I was in the south of France wondering what the hell I was doing and smiling.

Tiredness was working on me with the motion of the train and my eyes were closing now and then with thoughts of its good to meet 3 people who also have not trained for this. I was on a journey and it would take me as long as it took me I thought.

Upon arriving in St Jean realised I had said Buen Camino to my new friends and that it was Rain Man Xavier that had first said it to me. We all set of up the hill into the heart off the town where we would check in at the pilgrim's office.

Walking into the pilgrim's office felt good. My first official thing to do on the Camino. Met by two old guys who said wait a minute as they sat there finishing their lunch with their French Beret on. They were all smiles and soon were up asking me to sit. I filled out my Credential (official Camino passport) and I watched as he stamped it. The first stamp was in and there was a rush of excitement. These guys were great and explained that the Napoleon route the one over the top of the mountains

was closed meaning we had to take the valley route. Same length and still finishing at the place I am heading but a lot less dangerous. Places to eat were pointed out and other tips like where to stop for water and where I would be staying that night. Upon realising I was Scottish they both laughed and said one word RUGBY, the only French reply I knew was "merde". We all laughed and through broken English they told me how unlucky Scotland were in the Rugby.

Hungry, I ventured off on my own to find something to eat. The town is beautiful and the little place I ate in was just insanely lovely. Nothing fancy here just good food and wine. Wait hold the wine. That comes with the meal however I did say no thank you. I was happy to watch the older, I assume locals, enjoy their wine. Three courses later it's the pilgrim menu I set off to have a look at the municipal accommodation I'd be staying in and what the next thirty to forty or whatever days hold for me sleeping wise.

Well that's what I thought. As I headed to the refugio I met my fellow pilgrims and the two old rugby fans who were unloading boxes of scallop shells for the season. Before I knew it, I was involved in my first work and we were transporting thousands of shells to a safe place of storage till they would again see the light of day and a pilgrim would take a shell on their own journey. I wondered how many stories the shells I carried to the storage would be able to tell after the season. I knew the one I had had its own story so I could only imagine. After this I was invited back for tea by the gents that run the pilgrim office.

I signed into my accommodation for the night and the room has 16 beds of the bunk type. Very clean with power and a light at each bed. You don't get a choice of bed you're given one so I was happy that I got a bottom bunk. It's also really cosy so hopefully the sleeping bag does not have to be fully closed.

Once settled I took a walk all over the town of St Jean Pied de Port. What a very interesting place in that it was a main fort for the French when they were fighting with the Spanish. A large fort or "Citadelle "sits right above the place we are staying and dates back to the 1600's. It's now a college and I thought to myself what a unique place to go and learn.

It's a beautiful town and after returning for my walk I decided to have a shower and wash my undies and t-shirt that I have worn since leaving home. I was chuckling away to myself in the shower as I washed my stuff. Get used to it I thought.

I have also mastered the art of supermarket shopping. As I rarely do this at home I took a walk to the local superstore to try and buy my dinner. It was interesting as the only thing I understood was the picture and microwave symbol on one packet and the picture of strawberries and milk on the other. So, off I trotted back the refugio with my expertly bought goods. When I say expertly I pointed, smiled and said merci. All was good with microwave meal and when I took huge gulp of my refreshing strawberry milk I discovered that it was actually cream.

I painted my daily picture and chatted to some more pilgrims. I'm looking forward to starting the walk tomorrow. It's a tough day and 25 km uphill but I'm going for it.

*"Life's a Garden – Dig it" ~ Joe Dirt (couldn't resist this great quote)*

# Day 1, 26th February

## Camino Dream gets real, amazing and sore
## SJPDP to Roncesvalles

I was in bed by around 9.30/10pm last night however couldn't sleep. Some of my fellow Pellegrino's (pilgrims) were already sound asleep while a couple of the young ones sat in the eating area sampling the local wine and telling stories of why the Camino is for them. One girl from Germany, Luise, has already walked 1000 km from Switzerland and started five months ago. Quite amazing I thought as I lay in bed. It was warm so the mummy sleeping bag was set to the side and the provided blanket was enough. I eventually fell asleep and woke up around 5am. Everyone else was still sound asleep and no one was snoring. This panicked me quite a lot as I realised that there is always at least one heavy snorer and if no one else was snoring then did that make me the heavy snorer and the reason everyone was so sound asleep was that I had kept them awake all night.

At 6am I got up and went to the eating area to be greeted by an elderly lady who was a joy. All smiles and making me a cafe. The breakfast provided was simple. Coffee, bread, butter and strawberry jam. It was perfect and the wee woman pottered about cleaning and giving the warm smile and warm everything's going to be OK look. I contemplated when I would set off. The earlier the better I thought as it was over 26km today and I hadn't carried my rucksack more than 1km yet oops so my only concern was my two sore feet, sore knee and sore back that keep coming and going. Three areas not that important when walking I chuckled to myself. As Joe dirt would say "ya gotta keep on keepin on".

After breakfast and all the people in the refugio were up and about and there was a sense of excitement amongst everyone. All with their own reasons for being there and starting this journey. Eduardo the twenty-one-year-old Italian was ready and with a "Buen Camino" he was off into the dusk to start his pilgrimage. Twenty minutes later we spotted that poor Eduardo had left quite a few pieces of clothing in the drying room. Poor guy was going to need his stuff.

As instructed by my yogi friend Junie I completed a few sun salutations before lifting my rucksack to start my own journey. It was with the two girls Britt and Luise and we were off. On our way out of St Jean we ran into Lee. A young guy from Korea who does not speak any language that any of us speak and he was standing looking at a map. I had been to this crossroads the day before during my "explore of the city" so I pointed to Lee the way to go and he joined us. Now there were four of us and we were heading out of town. A little while later as we walked we saw a sad and frustrated looking Eduardo coming back. He was saying that he had left a lot of his clothes back at the refugio. The poor guy was well on his way and now returning. We said we had seen his things and off he went. After a few meters, I shouted "Eduardo" he turned to look at us and both Luise and I laughed and said it's OK as we have your clothes. We had split them between us knowing we would eventually run into Eduardo. It was great to watch his face turn from sad to unbelievable delight. Luise and I both smiled. Our good deed for the day complete. Now there were five of us on the way.

We started the slow climb through the valley, five pilgrims plodding our way up the valley towards the border of France and Spain. Passing through the small village of Arneguy, beautiful, on our way to Valcarlos. The walk was beautiful and I was looking up thinking I'm in the Pyrenees. We stopped in the mountain village of Valcarlos. It had taken us three hours to get to the place and it was time for a bite to eat and a coffee before heading of for the second half. The steep climb up the mountain was ahead and I was really excited about that – not.

After lunch I set off on my own as I wanted to listen to some music and go at my own pace. It was beautiful and although I was constantly climbing I was enjoying the walk. I knew a steep part was coming but I didn't realise how steep it was. The last 9km was a complete test on me. I can't say I seen much as my head was down and I was setting myself goals of 25m. Get there and it will be fine. Get to the pass over the top and you'll feel great. I walked and Ibaneta pass (3460 ft.) did indeed come into sight just at the same time as Coldplay's "Fix You" came onto my earphones. I swear it could not have been timed better. I was tired and sore but that song took me back to October and I will say without being embarrassed I cried at the top of the pass and was just so proud that I was here. Tears of joy and as I walked the last km or so down to the monastery I had a quite emotional trek. A million things flooded my head and I was in a good place. My Camino dream was now a reality in progress.

The monastery at Roncesvalles did not open till 4pm so two others who had caught up with me (I may be the oldest out of the group but I was still the first to the top it wasn't a race though) went for food and I drank five coca cola's that tasted like they were made in heaven. I swear they were just sublime. I also ate my Pellegrino dinner of pasta then pork. Two plates of which would have served all 3 of us. It kind of did as the others tucked into it along with their soup.

We checked into the accommodation and it's not as fancy as last night. The bunks are joined together so tonight I literally sleep next to some woman I've not even said hello to. And yes, that is a first for me. I wait for a shower as they are being used and then I intend to do nothing too much. My painting may be of a foot tonight. A basic foot at that. Day 1 complete, feeling proud and the journey has just started. Oh, I'm dreaming of a bath already. I think I'd pay just for a bath right now. Oh, and my fellow pilgrims are now all here safe, sore and happy. Oh, and thanks to my dad who bought me my walking poles. I had not used them till today and I now swear by them. Incredibly brilliant when going up and down. Here are a few words I received today that I love from my great friend Amanda.

> "Your mind will always believe everything you tell it. Feed it faith. Feed it truth. Feed it Love."

# Day 2

## There's snow way to that place
## Roncesvalles to Zubiri

Last night I had been tired but couldn't get to sleep. I was in bed by 8.30 however that was down to the factor that I was not only tired but the inside of my thighs were covered in Vaseline due to chafing. I did chuckle as I had not expected that. The room was compact with sixteen of us and most came into the room around 10.30pm so there was no chance of sleep. It's funny listening to many different foreign languages trying to unpack in the dark.

I woke up at around 6.30am and immediately checked to see if said chafing was OK. Sighs it was. I had woken up a couple of times during the night and no snoring other than my new friend a foot away. This morning I was told there were a couple of snorers. So, for a second time when I'm awake, I hear no one else snore, therefore, I have concluded I must be one of the snorers. I asked but was politely told it was a couple of people but no one will point the finger. Just tell me if it's me I say.

I came out of the room to look out the window at the morning light and was a tad shocked to see it chucking it down with snow. The murmurs of its snowing (not snoring) quickly consumed the room and people were sleepily getting out of bed to go and look at this white stuff as if it was a joke that they were hearing this.

First things first I thought. Get some Vaseline on the bits below as a preventative measure and get packed and ready to go at first light. It was about 24 km to the next stop and the way it was snowing I wanted to get down the mountain sooner rather than later. Packed and ready one of the girls said to me "snow trousers?" "No wonder your pack is big. I looked outside at the weather and then at her denims and thought yes waterproof trousers. I now did not doubt my packing. The start of day two and I was requiring my waterproof stuff and I absolutely needed the Vaseline for you know where.

Britt and I were the first to leave and we set off and the first stop was at a sign that tells you it is 790 km to Santiago. Kilometers is a foreign language to me so it doesn't seem that far. It's like euros or dollars. This Coca Cola is only €20. I'm like really. Is that expensive.

3km into the walk we came to the village of Burguete. Beautiful little place however it's where witches used to have their coven and where nine poor ladies were burned at the stake in the town square. I did think I wouldn't mind the fire going now as it's so cold. Without the witches, of course. There was a cross for some sort of protection against the witches that was interesting. Stopping at a cafe we ate a breakfast of the freshest pastries and coffee then set out in the snow all smiles and ready to enjoy the snow. That enjoyment would change later.

There was now a group of five of us at a crossroads in the town with the sign for the Camino pointing one way. When I asked what the concern was the group said that due to the heavy snow they thought that it was safer to stick to the road than cross over the hill using the main Camino path. I thought they may be correct as I headed down the Camino path. I mean what could go wrong?

As I was passing over the bridge out of town on the Camino path I looked behind to see where my fellow pilgrims were and realised that they had actually all started along the main road. I thought to myself that it's only 3.4km (1/2 a mile I think in my terms) to the next village and the path was, while snowy, spectacularly beautiful. Crossing over small rivers I looked behind me now and then expecting to see some people however it was only my footsteps stretching back as far as I could see. I thought about the little card Helena my friend had given me when I came out of hospital. It is called Footprints and it was one of the things I put in my wallet to walk the Camino.

This was beautiful and as I came to the hill I had read about there was a Camino marker to say what way to go. Remembering the last words of the group of "the markers may be covered by snow" I thought ah this is easy as it was clear as day. Well when I say clear it had one arrow pointing one way and another arrow pointing the other way. Ah the paths must meet of course I thought. I headed up the hill and the snow was getting deeper and my smile getting wider. At the top of the hill it started to confuse me a little. The choice of three very snow-covered paths. I was trying to remember what I had read about the way the shell pointed on the road to Santiago. I remembered wrong. So looking at the obvious wide path covered by snow going one way I decided to go the other way.

Setting of down this path I was hitting the trees with my walking poles and I thought I was in a winter wonderland. When I tapped one of the branches the snow would fall off releasing the pressure and the branch would spring up. I was doing this fast and the branches were flying up with clouds of snow exploding like a millennium fireworks display. As this happens it created a pathway and I was sure I was going the correct way. I was even more sure when through the mist of snow, I saw the blue and yellow sign of the Camino on a post. Proud of myself I looked at the post and noticed that a set of footprints was heading up the hill. Wait I thought. This hill looks like the same hill that I just climbed a while back. Those footprints look awfully like my own footprints. Reality set in and I had managed to go around in a huge circle. I had got lost and that was with markers. If I set up the hill again and now confused as to why these markers were pointing the wrong way I thought maybe I have it the wrong way. This time at the top I turned right and into a path I thought was correct and headed down. Half way down and with a contingency plan of going back to the town I saw someone walking towards me. OK so I'm walking the wrong way but I will soon find my way I thought. The conversation with the local Spanish man was simple. I said "Santiago" he said that way (the way I was going) I said "Espinal" the next village and he laughed and said " three hundred metres" There was the town but a few feet away. I had spent 30 mins going around in circles like a kid on a merry go round and the village was right there. I wonder if people do that a lot or was it just me?

Through the village I went and left on the path to head up yet another hill. I could see a Pellegrino ahead of me and I soon caught up with Eduardo and then Britt who was coming back down the hill. She said that at the top it was up above her knees deep and no markers so the decision was made to take the road to the next Camino entry point. Meeting a girl from Korea we used sign language to turn around and in no time Brit and I were heading up the main road in what were now horrendous conditions and my pace was brisk. With sixteen or so km to go and the snow not easing up it was now starting to turn into a let's get to shelter type day. Brit who had her jeans on with tights underneath was obviously wet but plodding on and we joined the Camino path at the top of a hill. Downhill we went and we were now both getting wet and when we arrived at the village of Viscarret there was nothing open so we kept moving.

The next few kms were not short and as we were lower the snow was very sleety and when climbing up a hill the path was a river coming down and when going down the same. Imagine walking up and down a stream that was made of water and slush over and over.

6.4 km the sign said. That's not far in miles I thought but I swear it was the longest 6.4 km I've ever walked and I gave Britt some of my life story. Why do you not drink Iain? so I told her and then I spoke about love at first sight and that it is possible and we talked about if people have "the one" I believe so. We were now only 3 km from the destination and there was a coffee van just there in the middle of the snow. I had to have one which was huge mistake. After taking off my soaking gloves and trying to put them back on I realised that I could not feel most of my fingers. I was soaking and my hands frozen. I set of after Britt who couldn't stop at the coffee place. A steep descent into the village of Zubiri saw the snow turn to heavy rain.

We entered the village laughing at what a crazy 24 km that had just been and headed to see if we could find accommodation. A long story short and about an hour later we arrived at a private Albergue (hostel) where a couple of our Pellegrino friends were there also. Bliss. Taking a shower, I sat in it for a good twenty or so minutes and it was heaven. By far the best shower I have had in a long time. Everyone from the previous night started to arrive. Clothes all getting dried and stories of everyone's day being told around the dining area. We were all glad to be there.

All I had to wear was shorts and a jumper and I was hungry. The wee man who owned the Albergue said he would drive me and two others to a restaurant, which was amazing service, as it had started snowing heavily. We ate and he came back later and picked us up. Not only that he knew the person who owned the supermarket, that was closed, so he went and got the key so we could purchase some food for tomorrow. I had a little go at being a Spanish shopkeeper and was pretty good at it may I add.

*"Boldness has genius, power and magic in it." ~ Goethe*

*Day 2 - Lots of snow and kms*

# Day 3

## Sole searching – literally
## Zubiri to Pamplona

After I had finished writing the blog last night we all sat around and chatted. When I say all, I mean the group has yet again grown. Well they were there in Roncesvalles when I went to bed but the albergue we stayed in yesterday had twelve beds and was the only one open so our new group included Takka from Japan, Tiger and Lee from Korea, Peter from Poland and a couple from Mexico. It was fun as we all told stories about this and that.

I realised that my clothes were not drying in front of the fire as there were twelve sets of wet clothes. The owner of the albergue had a sign saying he would dry your clothes in a dryer for

€2 - that's like 4 pence in our moneyI couldn't understand why others would not want this but I paid the €2 and this morning as I watched others put on their wet clothes I was glad I was in dry ones. The albergue name was Rio Arga Ibaia and was beautiful. I came into the dining area this morning and the table was all set for breakfast for everyone.

Britt and Tiger were first to set off and I was a few minutes behind as I spent a bit of time trying to figure out how to actually wear a poncho. Clint Eastwood used to just fling one over his shoulder. It wasn't that easy but I wanted to give it a go. This game of fix the poncho continued for the whole walk today.

I set off on my own and the destination was Pamplona. Most famous for the running of the bulls. Looking forward to seeing the city I plugged in my earphones and thought that 21km was a nice day and so far it was only light rain.

I walked and this was my first full day on my own. The biggest light bulb OMG moment I had was this. My earphones always fall out and I'm forever balancing them in my ear. I for some reason changed the angle more facing forwardand they fitted my ear, sounded louder and didn't fall out. I swear I laughed and laughed that it has taken me, I don't know how many years, to figure out how simple earphones work. Seriously though. Music loud and clear I set off again through various quiet villages including Larrosoana, Zuriain and Arre.

Some guide book the others had stated that this was the "ugly" section of the Camino. As I walked and everything I looked at was brand new to me I could not think how wrong their guide book was. Walking along the banks of the Rio Arga for a lot of the way the snow and rain from yesterday was now obvious in that the normal quiet river was now hurtling down the valley. The snow from the previous day had made the headline news there was so much.

Walking into the outskirts of Pamplona, which is a fairly big city with around 200,000, you pass through a place called Arre that had very impressive waterfalls and an ancient bridge. I had to rest here for ten minutes as now my feet and legs were sore, very sore. I had not stopped and walked around four hours straight. Note to self take rests.

I moved off in the direction of the old town of Pamplona through some welcomed busyness of the outlying towns of Villava and Burlada. I was down to a slow pace as my feet and legs were so sore and I remembered an old guy passing and just smiling. That was enough to boost my energy for a bit and then a couple passed me and said "Buen Camino" at this point I literally felt like I was the only pilgrim out on the Camino. Now I just wanted to get to the Albergue and get my boots off. One thing that struck me is that if you look there was always a sign pointing you in the direction to go. Camino arrows are a lovely thing to see.

Entering over the old bridge and gate into the old city of Pamplona, I was at this point definitely sole searching. As in where were the soles of my feet? Walking up the hill through the gates I knew I was going slow when an old woman smoking a cigarette flew by me. Nobody likes a smartass I thought.

I checked into the Albergue for €8 and it is an old church. I was the third person for the day after Britt and Tiger. Taking my boots off was sublime, amazing, beautiful and then came the shower. Oh how I live for and love a shower. It was one of those ones that you press the button and it lasts a minute before pressing it again. Not for me as I just leaned my back against it for a good twenty minutes and it just kept going. I thought all I need is Cameron Diaz to rub my aching legs and life would be perfect.

Later I went out to the supermarket mini to grab some bread, chorizo and cheese and also bought a non-alcoholic beer. That was insanely great also. I sat and ate some food with Tiger the South Korean and it was good to hear his views on the North and about his compulsory two-year army duty he has to do. He is here to complete the Camino before the army.

Fernando, our Spanish pilgrim, is a really nice guy who has just finished his medical degree and is our official restaurant guide. Next on the menu tonight was tapas. Not until I had loaded the washing machine first. We walked through the streets of Pamplona and it is a beautiful city. I walked up the street the Bulls run down and it looks so different from what I saw on the tv. It seems smaller and narrower. I need to look again. At a bar, I sampled three different dishes of tapas, which were lovely and I left the group to head back to the albergue. I was tired and wanted to rest.

"Be the change you want to see in the world." ~ Gandhi

# Day 4

## My Spanish improves kind of
## Pamplona to Puente la Reina

Last night it was the longest sleep I've had which I was surprised at as the place we were staying was an old church and the cloisters were lined with bunk beds. Again, more people are joining the Camino and a few extra bodies were with us. I laughed this morning as someone said it was creepy due to no one snoring. So, as I slept for a good seven hours then maybe it's not me that's the snorer. It was a nice place for €8. I did have to calm down at one point as I was tired and put my washing on then something happened that it didn't spin then the dryer broke down, my shampoo burst over my toiletry bag meaning a clean of everything and then the blog that I'm using crashed with the day's notes in it. One by one I rectified these small issues that just seemed bigger as I was in a big church and sore feet. An hour later I was satisfied with achievements and went to bed. I even wrote a poem.

When your laying back
And your mind is full
And you're in a town
Famous for the bull

Your feet are throbbing
And your calves so tight
The toilets far
For peeing through the night

The mattress it sinks
And your back does to
Where you're going next
You have no clue

But yet I smile
And dream that's true
The place goes quiet
Sleep – that's my Q

Before I forget and no one believes me. I saw my first ever Spanish Snowman on the way into Pamplona yesterday. It made me smile. This morning I headed out of the quiet centre of Pamplona at around 8.20am with my walking companion Tiger. It was slightly wet and we were both prepared with our ponchos and waterproofs. The old town of Pamplona is beautiful however it soon opens up to a modern looking city with the hustle and bustle and tall buildings. Tiger the guy from South Korea and I started chatting as we headed out on the 25km journey to Puente la Riena. We were following the big shells that show the way of the Camino that are on the ground and we were talking and talking when I stopped and said, "Tiger there are no signs for the Camino". He laughed and said you're right. As we both stood there looking very obviously lost a kind Spanish lady came over and I just said that magic word "Santiago" she smiled and pointed up the street and said "reet yeeellow" I said many thanks in Spanish and we were in our way to turn right at the yellow sign and we were on "The Way" heading out of town towards Cizur Menor.

Tiger was an interesting chap and he was telling me that after his two years in the army he was going to study as a priest for eight years. His thoughts on theology and his "very left" (as he described them) views of the church were not only interesting but kept us chatting for the first 6 km. I think this young guy will make a difference to the world one day.

The landscape started to change and I knew that we had a hill ahead of us but my feet and legs were OK so with my music on I headed away ahead of Tiger towards the climb. I had my music on shuffle and it felt as if the music gods were just putting on a great tune one after the other and I was singing as I headed up hill through the literally sleepy village of Zariquiegui where I stopped at one of the water fountains that are in some villages.

I drank a lot of water as I had not yesterday and had promised myself to drink more today. Onwards I headed up the hill to Alto del Perdon. The climb up was not as bad as I expected and it was interesting to see the whole skyline is covered with wind turbines. The special thing about reaching the summit is there is a monument made of wrought iron that represents medieval pilgrims. It was made more famous I guess by the movie "The Way" and while it was blowing a gale it was amazing to stand there at the top and one way was the city of Pamplona and the other way the way I was going was a sea of green undulating fields. It looked beautiful looking over the valley and at all the small villages scattered throughout. One of which was my destination. Heading out of the wind and down the hill I still had around 11km to go and the ground was hard on my feet. The pain was coming but the grass was green and the path inviting and I trotted on and came upon a young girl I had not seen before. She stopped me and in broken English I discovered that she was walking in the opposite direction. I had heard of this and she asked me how far Pamplona was and I said 2.5 3 hours. As I walked away I realised it was probably more but she would get there. A little while and a couple of selfies later I was walking, albeit slowly, through some beautiful countryside. The strangest thing is when you go through these little villages I normally see not a person. Just me walking through villages and it feels like they were left in a hurry and the water is still boiling on the stove. Maybe they heard I was coming. In one village there was a monument that had the shape of a person cut out of it that I naturally went through and got stuck due to my rucksack. I asked others and they said they didn't go through it. I'm sure I was right in doing it even if I did look a bit daft. As Forrest says, "Stupid is as Stupid does" I think. Here I also saw something that proved young Scottish people have been speaking fluent Spanish for years without knowing it. Back home a vending machine is commonly known as "The Vendy" well guess what, in Spain, it's also called the "Vendi" same same. The next stop was the finish point for the day and my feet and legs were now agony and I swear if they could talk they were not being nice to me. There is always something fun and energising about walking into the village/town at the end of the day. My music was on and I was singing loud. My feet were happy knowing we were nearly there and burst out into a rendition of the famous opera song "o sole mio"

Takka and Lee were outside the albergue and waving along the street to me saying it's closed, it's closed. A few swear words passed through my mind then I got told a story that it actually opened in five minutes. Feet happy again. Takka told me the supermercado was open for another thirty minutes so away I went in search of food and I enjoyed the experience. A quick aside. Takka laughed and said the word Sumo when I was getting changed. What Takka from Japan didn't realise was that I was also aware of this international word for fat man. I looked at him and said you just call me fat. I think he was mortified so I just body slammed him sumo styleI didn't really. As walked into my home for the night Britt and Eduardo were at the checkout. I said "Hola" and Eduardo the Italian replied "bien" and you. Striding past the checkout I naturally came out with "muy bien gracias"(very well thank you). I could see the woman at the checkout looking confused and I knew she was thinking, he doesn't look Spanish, he's not dressed like a Spanish man but his fluent Spanish and incredible accent can only mean he is truly Spanish. With this in my mind I set off round the Supermarket in full Spanish mode saying "hola como estas"(hello how are you) to the butcher, then I went to the fresh bread area and pointed at one loaf of bread and said "una porfavor"(one please) I knew they all thought I was local, how could they not with my expert language and accent skills. I approached the checkout and before she could even say a word the "hola" and "plastico por favor " obviously meaning a plastic bag please fluently came from my mouth. Without a word the money was exchanged and as I was about to walk away I looked her in the eye and I froze. Panic consumed me and I could see my cover starting to crumble. She looked deeper into my eyes and I knew that she was picking me apart. She had found me out. She knew. The realisation was true. I couldn't remember the Spanish word for goodbye. The butcher and the baker and I think even the candlestick maker started to appear and the word "goodbye" came out of my now not so Spanish mouth. Disappointment slowly engulfed the ladies face like the cold mist I had seen coming down the Pyrenees and she just said, "adios." Shamefully I left as my feet laughed at my epic language fail. So close but yet so far, I laughed to myself.

Returning to the albergue I ate a large lunch of bread, cheese and chorizo and as always just now washed down with Coca Cola. I didn't mention the shower as while it was great it was not the best one yet and I'm now a shower snob. I will now judge places on the showers they have. I wonder if I should now have a shower at everyone's house I visit. Still a little hungry I headed out with my Spanish restaurant buddy Fernando, German Luise and Britt. The little place was amazingly beautiful and cheap. I had an omelette and potato brava before we headed back to drink some tea. Day 4 done and my guide tells me I'm now less than 700 km to go. Progress comes with time and small steps I thought.

> "The Universe is always speaking to us... sending us little messages, causing coincidences and serendipities, reminding us to stop, look around, to believe in something else, something more." ~ Nancy Thayer

# Day 5
## This little piggy said what's going on
## Puente la Reina to Estella

As I write this my current position and feeling is this. I roll my eyes back in a feeling of ecstasy as I soak my aching, and I mean aching, feet in the most beautiful yellow bucket of water I have ever seen. I was advised to put some salts in however I have not mastered the skill of going to the shops twice with sore feet. So today.

A good sleep again last night that I put down to a number of factors. My body's tired obviously, I didn't hear anything as I used my earplugs for the first time which worked a treat and the impromptu yoga session I held last night. I had everyone stretching and we all had a good laugh. Some really interesting characters. Pain wise I'm one of the best in that I just ache and I'm tight. There are some nasty blisters, ouch and poor Eduardo has a really bad knee. Luise the German girl, who is has walked over 1150 km already, also has a sore knee but she is smart. She takes her time every day and is last to the place we're staying. Always with some good tales.

Up and at them early as they say and I hadn't bought any breakfast as some do so I left with Britt to stop at the first cafe that sold coffee and pastries. A tiring 500m later my rucksack was off and as my mouth filled with wetness at the anticipation of what delights I had to choose from. With my regular "Cafe con leche" coffee with milk and a rather scrumptious looking pastry was winking at me. For a short while I sat quietly at the sheer greatness of the moment. The sun was out and my stomach was full. Time to head out of town for the 22km walk to Estella.

As I looked back the town of Puente la Reina looked beautiful in the morning light as Britt and I headed off and with tales of sore feet and blisters it was not long before the morning clouds had worn off and there was sun shining on our faces. It has been a while since I had felt that warm glow radiate my skin and my thoughts were to take my jacket off however I could still feel a nip in the air so it stayed on.

The walk had been billed as an easy day by all of us first time Pellegrino's as we had studied our guidebooks and noticed that it was not hilly. So, after the last few days we set off full of chat and it was interesting to hear a little about Britt. I knew she had travelled in a few places with India being one. I wanted to know so asked her about her experience. She had been there twice with one time being for three months doing various pieces of work to help people write and give aid in various forms. I learned a personal lesson here during the conversation. I have never been to India nor have I been close to anyone who has worked there that would give me any sort of real understanding of life. Britt was explaining life and various things when I interrupted with "is it like our countries as in developing" She started to explain a whole bunch of her views and I thought to myself. Listen. Just listen. I had no experience and I realised I was letting my mind come to conclusions without any real knowledge of the country other than documentaries on the TV. I just listened and let her tell me about her three-month experience. It was nice to just really listen and stop my brain from trying to piece things together. I guess our minds can just make things up and we have to stop ourselves from making up wee stories when we think we know the answer but we actually really don't. Our minds trying to solve problems I guess.

"The way" was not so easy and soon we were climbing a very steep hill and as I moved further ahead I was walking through more beautiful Spanish countryside on my own. It really is stunning and as I walked through the first village of Maneru I stopped to look at some of the buildings. Maneru is linked some way with Knights Templar and the order of St John. I'm told that The Way has a lot of history with the Knights Templar.

Putting my music on I set off for next village of Cirauqui which was only about 3km away and sat on a piece of high ground. It was a stunning sight to walk to. Sitting high like a proud eagle overlooking the valley and towns below. On entering there was a slope up to the left that had a couple of huge standing stones on it at the entrance to a graveyard. It looked interesting however I decided not to head up to that and go into the village itself. There was a junction at the entrance to the village with two options to take and I couldn't see the usual yellow and blue marker for the Camino. However, my fellow Pellegrino Lee from South Korea was resting right there. He speaks pretty much zero English and I smiled and pointed at both directions. The international way of saying "what way?" He pointed straight ahead. I did the same and thumbs up and he thumbed up as well and off I set into the village. It was not long before I realised there were no markers for the Camino so I weaved my way through some narrow streets till I came to an open area with a map. A big spot with a "you are here" was on the map and I realised I was not on the Camino but close. Just as I was about to head in the right direction the bold Lee arrived from what is the correct way and smiled with his thumbs up. I laughed as one of two things had happened when I asked him for directions. Either he had no clue what I was pointing at and putting the thumbs up and that he just copied me to be polite and probably wondered where is that guy heading off to when the Camino is to the left OR Lee is from Glasgow and is on the wind up by kidding on he doesn't speak English and is having his own Camino joke fest. I bet it is the second one. Well I hope it is as that would be amazingly funny. We did take a few minutes to take a picture of the gate into the town then off Lee strode and I felt my stomach rumbling. Oh oh! I thought. Find the nearest toilet/restroom. Noting that I had only seen a public toilet once on the first day I quickly whipped out my........guidebook and got the phrase "Donde estan los servicios". There was one lady passing through the main square so I sprung my new Spanish phrase on her and she looked at me, smiled and said "servicios" and I said yes. She smiled again and just said "no" and walked away. Standing not knowing if I should laugh or cry I thought the next village it is as I'm still not ready to fertilise the farmers' fields just yet. The whole toilet thing is an interesting thing in the albergues as everything is shared so if you're shy about let's say noises then you need to get over that quick.

By this time Britt had caught up with me and we set off towards Locra which was a mere 5.7km away. I was moving a bit faster and I again found myself with my thoughts and music. I was thinking about some people and life. Just good thoughts about pops and my mum, Junie my friend and yoga teacher who is building a business that delivers her dream, Donna who has taken the brave step to move back to her hometown for a fresh start and how I hope I see her when I return, another friend who is taking up a health challenge. I was thinking about all these brave decisions people were taking every day to improve things for themselves and how they feel. Quite inspiring thinking of them all doing their things and being brave and taking risks.

Reaching the town of Lorca I asked the same question about the toilet to a local with the same response. I sat and drank some water next to a running fountain. Not the best when needing the loo. I had to at least pee so I set off out of town and found a bush to do what nature does and have the most satisfying pee I've had.

My feet were sore and they were now becoming the main focus. I headed through Villatuerta which was a small town of modern houses and took a wrong turn but soon found my way back in the Camino.

A sign said that the finish was only 2.4km away. Sometime later I discovered that this sign must be either wrong or I had started to lose it with my sore feet. I passed a donkey and said hello to it in Spanish. It just looked at me. I had the strangest thought looking at the animal. I was thinking this. My name is McKie so like "son of Kie" pronounced son of Key. If I was a mafia boss then would that make me Don Kie? Laughing at this I headed off to the town that was definitely longer than 2.4km.

Reaching the albergue is a great feeling as by this time my feet are just aching so much. I checked in for €6 and headed off to the supermercado for food. That was a challenge as it was a fifteen-minute walk however food was important I figured. I purchased pasta, sauce and chocolate pudding for about €8 and came back to the kitchen and cooked it all up. When the group started to arrive, I had a bowl of pasta with bread and meat ready for them if required. I fed five people this way. My good deed for the day done. I have to mention the shower. It was bliss. It is the first one where you can just leave it on and it has a hook for the wall so you can just stand under it. Again, I was in there a good twenty minutes. I may even have another one.

The town is beautiful and I had a short visit around a museum "The Carlism Museum" which is across the street from the albergue. Interesting and kind of like the Jacobite revolution back home. Seemingly there is still some guy in the Netherlands who says he is the real king of Spain. Interesting but I had to get back to rest my feet.

*I rest my feet before I greet*
*I smile at why they're sore*
*I rest the meat and take a seat*
*I must sound like a bore*

"Nothing not even pain lasts forever,
if I can just keep putting one foot in front of another,
I will eventually get to the end." ~ Kim Cowart

# Day 6

## A massage a day should be a must
## Estella to Los Arcos

Another great sleep last night of at least six and a half hours. The evening was nice with lots of food kicking about the table. Lots of people headed off to bed however I don't go to sleep much before midnight so it was Luise the German, Alexandro and his wife Elea from Mexico who were left in the communal area. The lights all went off at ten and the four of us were left in the dim light that was coming from the "vendi". Then after a few minutes that went off too. We laughed and Luise went and retrieved her head lamp. Elea went to the stairwell that had some light to write her diary, Alexandro was playing on the internet and Luise sat next to me and put an earphone in my ear and one in hers and said listen. I was met with the sweet gentle sound of some Italian classical music. Luise started writing her diary under the red light from her head lamp. I surfed the net and we were silent for a long time in the darkness with a dim red light and soothing music. It was a most relaxing time. An hour or so later the other two said their good nights and soon after I did also. A lovely end to another lovely day.

Waking up I do what I automatically do now and move my

feet. Stepping out of bed gently I take a few minutes to stretch them and then they felt good to go.

Thinking about sleeping I'm pretty positive I woke myself up snoring just one big snort. Well I think I did but again my sleeping buddies said they heard nothing. I feel like I deserve and want to be the snorer. Maybe I'll fake it. There is a joke there I'm sure.

Heading off up the old streets and past the museum from last night we headed out of Estella on our 21.5km trek to the town of Los Arcos. We did stop at a petroleum station for coffee. That is interesting as the petroleum station has a coffee bar and a booze bar in it. So theoretically you could make your local petrol station your local drinking establishment. You could get gassed in the gas station. I also saw a guy buying beer and it was before 9am. Seemingly the law has no problem with that. The three of us were now refreshed with coffee and we met Luise, Alexandro and his wife Elea outside and we headed for a special stop they had all been talking about.

As we headed out of town my thoughts were with Eduardo the lovable Italian guy who had hurt his knee and that morning was debating what to do. All I knew when we left was that he was not walking that day. Moving on out of town and it wasn't long before everyone was talking and getting excited and we strode up a hill toward the ancient Benedictine Monasterio de Irache with the Fuente del Vino. The Fuente del Vino is quite famous as it is a tap on the wall that when you turn it on the bright red liquid that is wine pours freely into the awaiting cups and shells of any pilgrim that so desires. The "troops" we're excited by this and Takka from Japan was already at the fountain of love with his Coke bottle filled with wine and his litre water bottle had a rather darkish looking liquid in it. He said that it was the Coke from the Coke bottle. I laughed and said sure. The team were soon filling their shells and vessels of wine and loving their 9am wine tasting. It was great to watch the excitement and listen to their stories of drinking wine at different times. The fountain of wine would have, at one time, been a place where I would have drunk and drunk. And this time was no different other than one detail. I drank my fill from the right-hand side tap that dispenses the purest of pure chilled fresh Spanish spring water and it was still a fantastic experience. It did pass through my mind how a free-flowing wine font would go down back home. I think people would make pilgrimages just to the font if that was the case.

Moving onwards through the village of Irache we climbed the hill towards the village of Azqueta that then rises again to the high point of the day Villamayor de Monjardin which gave great views over the valley we had just came through. I stopped at a covered well that is like a plunge pool and I'm sure people must dive in on a warm Spanish afternoon. After the climb up I removed my rucksack and enjoyed a rest with some well-deserved squares of chocolate. The bonus of walking a lot every day is that I'm eating nice treats and not worrying about it. Having said that I'm eating rather healthily. No fried breakfast here.

I was on my own again and was thinking these small villages each have their own unique beauty yet with the same styling. The way down again and the fields were green and open. Lots of little vineyards pop up alongside small patches of olive trees, both of which are prepared and ready for the years growing. As I did I passed some happy Pellegrino's just hanging out relaxing.

My feet were still doing OK and Britt had caught up and we entered our destination of Los Arcos. A small village of around 1600 people and a declining population. The albergue we were going to stay at was closed however other people we saw pointed out another and we checked into the quirkiest and dare I say coolest place we've stayed at.

Being hungry I went to the local shop and bought some pasta and the wee lady told me this was her home-made tomato and olive pasta sauce. She then said do I want some of her very own cow cheese that she has made. Well of course I did and she sliced of a slither if this cheesy delight. It was sensational to say the least. I went back to the albergue and prepared all the pasta that fed 5 of us again. It's cheap and brings a smile to some hungry faces.

The albergue had a sign offering massage and I asked how much it was. €10 for twenty-five minutes. I was down to my boxers and on the table before the money hit the masseuse's hand. It was bliss and I thought I should really get this done more often. Luise my German friend was walking by and I treated her to a massage also. She has walked from Switzerland and I thought you deserve a treat.

Later we headed to the supermarket to grab some snacks however it was still closed. The group said we'd go into the church in the main square to see while we waited. I don't think I can put into words the sight that met my eyes as I entered what I thought was a small village church. It was like nothing I've seen before with gold coloured and I'm sure gold alters, tapestries and unique stone work. The organ had faces painted on the open parts of the tubes so that it looked like the sound was coming out of their open mouths. There was a young monk praying in his robes and I simply stood for quite a while trying to take it all in. This was a massive surprise. I walked around and looked at the detail. Alexandro the man who is a theologian from Mexico even said to me that this was special. I had left my phone at the albergue charging so could not take a picture. I will try tomorrow when I pass in the morning. It's incredible.

Tomorrow we will try and do around 28km but I will go with what my feet tell me. Some of the group headed on today and I don't know if I'll see them again but it was good to know them.

What an amazing day of sights and surprises like the church. The biggest surprise was when we reached the albergue our friend Eduardo was there after catching the bus and resting his knee.

> *"You don't choose how you're going to die. Or when. But you can decide how you're going to live now."* ~ Joan Baez

*Britt, Luise and Fernando*

# Day 7

## When on the Camino Theology is awesome
## Los Arcos to Viana

We were asked to go to our beds at 10.30pm as it was lights off. I was thinking to myself that I will not get to sleep but within twenty minutes I was sound asleep and was there till about 6.30am. At least seven hours which is amazing. I'm surprised that I'm getting by with one pillow and the sleeping bag. I can't even imagine the luxury of a double bed and a bath now. It's like a dream. Maybe I'll have a spa day when I'm home.

I had booked the breakfast this morning and it was the typical one that you get. Bread, jam, butter and coffee all for a bargain €3.50. Full up I heard that it was raining so the rain gear was put on and I was ready to go. I had said goodbye to Britt who was intending to go further and a couple of the group had also gone ahead last night. Others in the group were wanting to go further today also. I was in no hurry to rush the Camino. Off I set and I wanted to look at the church but ten minutes later I was walking down the street and I realised I had left my walking poles. Back I went and picked up the poles and headed back towards the church as I wanted to take some pictures. Who forgets two big poles anyway? I reached the church in

Los Arcos that I had been immensely impressed with last night with the intention of taking some good pictures. It was closed however there was a picture board outside that I snapped. It really was amazing.

Luise passed by and I started walking with her out of town. I had a moment and due to forgetting my poles I thought I better check I have my passport and wallet. Rucksack off and checked. All was good and Luise and I headed towards the edge of town. Wait I said. She asked what is wrong. My head was shaking and I was laughing as I explained that when I checked my wallet I had put my poles against the wall and they were still there. Not even out of the town and I had forgotten them twice. Who forgets their poles twice? I collected them and caught up with Luise and we chatted about this and that.

We soon caught up with Alexandro and Elea and Alexandro and I walked ahead and started talking. Alexandro is from Mexico and is a Theologian. What a remarkably interesting man. He is well known I assume within the church in Mexico and had a fall out with a cardinal so is in the bad books with them for let's say speaking his mind. We were discussing loads of things and the politics around religion including corruption and power that is perceived and is true. I asked him about the Vatican and he told me that the many times he had been there that the best place for him was the chapel of tears and he told me the story of how the Pope goes there to pray after being made Pope. He talked about going to study in classes by the old Pope. I can't remember his name but the German one that resigned. I asked if he had ever had a chat with him and he said of course. I asked Alexandro so when he was Pope did you ever have a one on one chat with him and he just said yes. I asked what about and he said they talked about theology. So here I am walking the Camino with a Theologian who sits with Popes and cardinals. I'm totally consumed with his chat and we talked and talked for kilometre after kilometre. I had wanted to know more about St. James for which the Camino de Santiago is all about. I deliberately didn't read up on this before I left as I figured I'd learn along the way. Who better to learn from I thought? So, St. James it turns out was one of Jesus's twelve disciples and one of the closet to him. We talked

well Alexandro told me of the story of St James and how the walk we were doing was one of the most important pilgrimages in the world. He explained to me how the name Santiago came about and that Compostela was "Field of stars" it was a really interesting and fascinating chat. He's a naturally very smart guy but is just so easy going. I talked about Bonnie Prince Charlie and the 45's and Alexandro mentioned yes "the young pretender" I laughed to myself as I thought this Mexican guy knows more about Scottish history than I do and he's just humouring me. That's when I started to tell him how I was actually the last king of Scotland and we must have walked a good km as I explained why I was. He did laugh a lot. What an amazing couple of hours that was.

During the walk we passed through the small village of Sansol and stopped for coffee and a banana. After seven days I'm learning to take a break from continuous walking and the four of us chatted to the three Dutch women who are doing the same pace as us. My feet while still sore are happier with these breaks. After our snack it didn't take long to reach the small but picturesque village of Torress del Rio which is the home of the impressive Iglesia de Santo Sepulcro which is an Octagonal church that is linked to the Knights Templar. As with many churches it was locked however a nice wee note said if you called the custodian they would come and open it up for €1. There was no need as another picture board gave me the inside shot and history. A beautiful looking building.

Alexandro and his Elea met while on the Camino and we stopped by the albergue where they stayed and met for the first time, I think. It's nice to see them chat about places they saw, when they met and walked along this ancient route. My romantic side was loving it.

Moving onwards we navigated the Camino and we all chatted about various things and experiences on the Camino. Luise told how she had been propositioned while in France and the couple talked about how they had been travelling from last June. They started walking at the top of Norway. Not all the way to here as they flew here and there but they also walked the other Camino from Seville to Santiago in September. I am definitely the Camino virgin in the group.

The town of Logrono was 13 km ahead however I was not going there as my feet were starting to say stop soon and the smaller town of Viana was only a couple of kms away. The four of us decided that we were going to stay there. I had already had a voice message from the amazing Eduardo that the rest of the group were heading to the big town. That's the way the Camino works. One day you're chatting to people and the next day they're gone and you don't know if you'll see them again. It's great to meet them though.

The town of Viana was upon us and I had left my poles for a third time at a stop but quickly realised before it was too late and I thought only you Iain could forget something three times in one day. The town is pretty as you enter through a gate into the old section. It's an important town as this is the burial place of Cesar Borcia who was a famous/infamous general in his time. I believe he was ruthless and Alexandro told me the story of Cesar Borcia. I looked him up. It's an interesting story.

A shower later and my bag unpacked. We shared a washing machine to clean clothes and sat around the communal table eating bread and cheese. Tiger appeared as did the Australian couple so some of the group are still about. A rest, then time for dinner I thought. Five of us set out for dinner however the places were closed. Immediately I announced I'd cook dinner and before you could say "Jamie Oliver watch and learn" my little basket was full of ingredients to serve five and all for less than I'd have paid for my dinner in a restaurant. The others bought a few wee things and we headed back to the albergue.

It's great in the accommodation as it's only the seven of us who all know each other. I sat my friends down and set about cooking up a storm. Then served them desert and washed the dishes. Don't ask me why but I'm enjoying helping these tired souls by cooking them a bit of food.

Day seven has been a fantastic day. I didn't push myself to go any further than I thought I should. I rested when I wanted and I loved the chat. They all keep laughing at my continuous bad jokes so that's a plus. I have learned new things and seen again beautiful places. Tomorrow I don't know where I'll be but I know I'll savour every minute.

"It always seems impossible until it's done." ~ Nelson Mandela

# Day 8

## Moments of content
## Viana to Navarette

Retiring to bed last night let me spend another night in dream heaven. I slept pretty good with the odd toss and turn and woke up around seven. There was only the seven of us in the place so the usual routine of making breakfast and packing your rucksack commenced. I usually buy breakfast, a pastry and coffee, however I had some Coca Cola and a chocolate pudding left from last night that I had. Breakfast of champions I thought.

The Australian couple who are retired, I think, were away first. His name is Iain and his mum is from Glasgow so that is good conversation. They are on the Camino as it is on a list of things they want to do. Great energy and nice people. I set off around 8am on my own for the 22km walk to the town of Navarrete. Viana was a lovely town and steeped in history. The night with just the seven of us and cooking had made it a fun night.

The weather was around 3 C and the sun was peeking through the last of the sleepy clouds letting me know that it would soon come to visit. My feet were feeling good and I headed out of the town towards the city of Logrono which I could see in the distance. This is a large town of 155000 and the capital off the new region I was heading to. The region of course was Rioja. Famous for its sensational wine. I picked a good time to quit drinking I thought looking into the distance. I'd always loved a good glass of Rioja and I chuckled to myself as I recalled a time when pops, uncle Sandy and I drank a good amount of Rioja wine and I will always say that other than its unique taste it is the wine that gets the good stories flowing. It did that night.

The town was about 10km away and I spent time listening to music and thinking of this and that. The scenery of mountains far off to my right and vineyards all around me was beautiful. At one point the Oasis song Champagne Supernova came on and I stopped and took a picture. It was a surreal but amazing moment.

This time of day and with no sore feet my thoughts will wander to any number of subjects. I thought of my son Cameron and wondered if I'd ever get to tell him about this and how I ended up here. That's something I will share with him if I ever see him again. I did think and hope that he is a happy wee guy. I'm sure he is.

The scenery and the way the sun was shining at times was like a dream. I'd be walking and my music would be on and I'd look left and it would be like I was walking through a movie scene. Mother nature was sprinkling small doses of her very own unique happiness especially for me. I stopped a few times just to breathe in the moment. I can't describe it. Mother nature in her own beautiful way was saying everything is OK. I'm tearing up writing this. It was a feeling of content I can't describe.

I stopped to look at what I can only describe as a spider's nest and as I was doing this Alex, Elea and then Luise caught up and we all had a discussion as to what it was. An interesting debate ensued as we moved on but I'm positive it's a spider's nest. Heading off toward the city again we were all talking about this and that and as we drew closer you can tell it's a big town as the graffiti started however some of it was quite amazing. We crossed into the region of Rioja and into the city of Logrono. I was now getting hungry and a coffee was definitely what this Pellegrino wanted. On the way into town there was an old lady outside a house with a table. There were some trinkets for sale on the table and she said to us would we like our credentials stamped. We said yes and she was lovely wishing us well and "Buen Camino". While talking to her obviously happy dog who was wagging its joyous tail every time the old lady spoke to it. There was a warmth to her and off we set and I said to the others that I liked the old lady and she had a great idea in sitting outside saying hello to the Pellegrino's rather than sitting inside all day. Luise pulled out her guide book and showed me a picture of the old woman. She sits there every day and stamps any pilgrim's passport who wants it. She doesn't try and sell you she just wishes you well. Here is the even more amazing part. Her mother done this before her. Two generations of women who must have wished many pilgrims a good way. Incredible.

The city is big and we visited the church of Santiago which was magnificent. There was a huge sculpture of St James on a horse wielding a sword on top of the church and Alexandro was able to give me the history of how there was an order of St James. Kind of like the Templars as in they were warrior monks. There was a lot more history he told me.

As we walked through the city it became very obvious that the people here were very friendly with many saying Buen Camino to us as we walked down the street to arrive at a coffee shop. I love these wee places and I ordered my cafe con leche and some tapas type food. I was hungry and the potato omelette thing tortilla I think there called. OMG.

The walk out of Logrono and then the country park is quite deceiving as you walk a lot of kms before getting out of the town and then halfway around the country park. The whole way was concrete which is sore on the feet and we plodded along and took a rest where for the first time I lay on the ground with my head on my rucksack and let the sun warm my face while at the same time the chill from the ground was saying don't lie here too long. I headed off on my own with music on again and as I looked back I could see that Luise and Tiger were also having some "me" time. The walk through the vineyards took me to the highest point of the day and to my surprise our destination was well in sight and looked a short walk away. It was only about 3.5km. Off down I set and laughed at someone who had painted doggy footprints with an arrow. A little reflection of some dogs who have maybe also walked the Camino. As I was on the outskirts of town I waited for Luise who was not far behind and we looked around some ruins that used to be a hospital and albergue for pilgrims dating right back to 1185 however it was demolished in the 19th century due to the wars and lack of money.

The albergue we were going to stay in was closed so as the others were quite a bit behind Luise and I bought some tapas and coffee and we sat in the sun and waited for the others. This was just amazing after a 22 km walk. A while later and Luise with a glass of wine consumed we decided we had not seen the others so we headed towards the next albergue. Just then Alexandro and Tiger both messaged me to ask where we were as they were in yet another albergue. I laughed and thought next time just check in Iain and they will find you.

We checked in to be greeted by everyone and it was as usual great to see everyone and we got our beds ready and relaxed, showered and ready for dinner. The shower in this albergue is the worst one so far and as it's down the hall it sucked a bit and I realised I had forgotten my micro towel and had to shout down the hall please bring me my towel to the others amusement. They thought it was hilarious.

A lovely day and a lovely dinner. Day eight done and who knows what experiences to come.

"No one has ever become poor by giving." ~ Anne Frank

*Luise, Elea, Alexandro, me, Iain and Trish(Australia) and Tiger*

# Day 9

## I spoke to an Angel today
## Navarette to Azorfa

Last night we all sat at the dinner table for nearly four hours and I treated myself to a hamburger with salad and a dessert of flan which was washed down with three pints of Coke while the others had the Pellegrino dinner washed down with bottles of Rioja. Again, I thought my dad and uncle Sandy would love it here with this delicious wine I was told it was delicious obviously. The owner of the place told us that the little village exported seven million bottles of wine in 2015. That blew my mind and it's also cheaper than Coke. The rest chatted and I painted and wrote this. Our room was only five of us as the Australian couple had shelled out a whopping €2 each for a private room with their own shower. Luxury at its best. We had fun and suddenly the five of us were sitting around my bed as I preached my life story and thoughts to a priest to be, an insanely clever guy that speaks with popes and the very smart women. It was fun though as I drank my Coke and we laughed so hard that it was like a high school dorm. There was a school or a college group in the albergue and we joked that the young ones would ask for the oldies to be quiet. Midnight came as did heavy eyes and I flew off into dreamland.

The morning we were up later than normal as breakfast was served at eight. It was a delicious pastry and coffee for €2.50. They even asked me if I wanted orange juice and I did. It was so nice. Then he said OK that's €4 for breakfast. A bit cheeky I thought but it was delicious. I found a way to carry the rest of my Coke and bread I had bought and thought I should send this idea to Berghaus (the make of my rucksack and boots) both of which are amazing so far.

A quick photo outside and it was time to leave the extremely quiet town of Navarrete and walk the 23 km towards Azofra.

We set off out of town and it was freezing cold. It was 3 C and the wind was making it feel colder. As we left the town we ran into Iain and Trish the Australian couple who were adding some layers due to the cold. It just so happened we were stopped at a graveyard. The front of it looked impressive and familiar. It turns out that the hospital for pilgrims that we had seen the day before and was demolished that they took the front of it stone by stone to this new location and re built it. It looks exactly like the diagram I had seen the day before. A few selfies and the magnificent seven were on our way.

Within minutes we were spread out into our own pace and Iain, Alexandro and myself were chatting. In what seemed no time at all we were at the place where we had an option to go straight on or go into the town of Ventosa. As some waited I was on up the road to another sleepy village and climbed the steep road and stairs to the church that was secretly holding onto a view that was breath-taking. I waved at the dots, who were Pellegrino's, in the village. When I came down I told them of the view and that they should go up. One asked if I had taken a photo and I said yes. That will do me then. I liked the patter.

We all went into the only bar in the town and the owner was so friendly. Everyone ordered coffee and a couple of us ate the tortillas. It was a lovely stop and the owner wanted a picture of all of us. I have been telling the group that I'm actually the last king of Scotland and that sometimes people recognise me so that's why they say hello to us. When he wanted a picture I just looked at them and said you see. They are now all calling me the last king of Scotland which I am of course.

Off we set and I headed away on my own with the UK top forty from before Christmas primed and ready to play. Walking over the top of the hills the wind was fierce and it was even colder. The snow topped mountains were off to my left and the next town of Najera was 10k ahead. The scenery was beautiful with vines planted in every conceivable place and wineries dotted through the landscape. The music was good even though there was a constant whistle from the wind past my invincible earphones.

Najera was only a few km away when I caught up with priest to be Tiger. He hadn't stopped as he was slower with blisters and just kept going. He is a great guy and likes that we are all open about lots of things and likes that I tell a few jokes that he says people won't do around him back home as he's studying to be a priest. We soon reached the town and stopped at the first cafe to eat more tortillas and drink coffee while we waited for the others who showed up fifteen minutes later.

Refreshed we set off again and stopped at the monastery that is the burial place of the kings and queens of the region. It was closed but we got a quick history lesson from Alexandro and we were off for the final 7 km to our goal town of Azofra.

I was ahead again with my music on and was enjoying the fact that I was heading along at a steady pace with the trusty Justin Bieber playing away in my ears. Well it was the top forty however it seems he has about 20 songs in it. The pace was good and I was enjoying entering a town and at a pace of enjoyment without crippling sore feet. I was here and the walk had been great. Beautiful scenery, deep thoughts, funny stories, great food.

It was now I met an Angel. We went to the municipal albergue and there were a lot of people with kids there. Alexandro spoke with a young guy who was not so awesome and he told us it was closed as it was hired out for the locals and to go to the other albergue in town. Off we went and went into the not so great looking place but it had eight beds and a shower but no one there. We called the hospitaler (the person who runs an albergue) who arrived within minutes. An older gent who walked in chatting and chatting in Spanish. He was yapping away to Alexandro, the only one who spoke the language, for quite a while. I was getting a bit like OK what's going on. I just want a shower I thought. The man stopped turned and looked at us all with a smile and Alex explained that we could either stay in the place or this guy would open up the big albergue where the party and not so nice guy was. He explained that he was at our service and wanted every pilgrim to be treated the same. He insisted on us sitting and taking it easy, he was excited as we chose to stay in the more modern place. He was just such a warm amazing old guy who wanted us to be happy and comfortable. His name is Angel. Formalities completed and Angel escorted us through the town like we were kings and queens in a precision. I thought to myself that maybe Angel has lived here all his days and he was proud of his town and at that moment he was proud to be leading us through it. We came to the turn to go to the albergue and Angel pointed forward shouting Santiago. We kept going to hear Angel pissing himself at his joke of sending us all the wrong way. We all laughed with him and headed to the albergue. Angel soon took care of the young guy and we were in. Rooms of two. Angel was by far my highlight of the day. This guy just wanted to help the pilgrims and did so with enthusiasm, humour and quite obvious love of helping. He is truly an angel.

A fantastic shower later and I'm sharing a room with Tiger the future priest. Never thought I'd say that in my life. We all sat out in the hallway with the sun warming our tired bodies and relaxed. I was quite content. Heavy eyes I started to write this when I heard boom, boom, boom. What's that noise in a village with a population of 250 and declining I thought. Food was required so we all set of to the supermarket as the boom, boom, boom got louder we could hear the DJ voice and the laughter. Turning the corner, we were met by a small but very loud street party going on. All the adults were crowded in a bar while the kids and some Pellegrino's got down to some dancing. I done the YMCA proud with some great moves and danced to some Mexican song under a Spanish sky. A beautiful day and we were all invited to dinner by the college group that have arrived and cooking dinner. Saturday nights are meant to be just like this. I end with the poem I wrote for my wonderful Camino friend from Germany Luise that I read out at dinner.

My Camino Dream it started blank
And when I saw her my pure heart sank
Her reddish hair and sparkling eyes
I never wanted no more goodbyes

However, a stripper is what she is
And every man she gives a kiss
A stamp a day for some poor man
It's what I want but don't think I can

So Luise, with your bright red hair
I only want you to just take care
And if he's short or if he's tall
When you stop the stripping give me a call.

(Luise is not a stripper to clarify and it was just a bit of fun)

"Life isn't about waiting for the storm to pass...It's about
learning to dance in the rain." ~ Vivian Greene

# Day 10

## Surprise after surprise, I'm grateful
## Azofra to Granon

Last night flung a few surprises as every day seems to do. In a good way. We had eaten some bread cheese and sausage and the college folks came into the communal dining area to prepare their dinner. The lecturer was talking to the students in Spanish and telling them where we were from and that we were walking The Way. Not long after fresh cooked eggs, bread, chorizo and chips were delivered to our table compliments of the Spanish school. It was delicious and the kindness was quite lovely. After dinner I painted Luise's face and she painted mine as you have to amuse yourself somehow. It gave us a giggle. At one point, quite late, the sound of a marching band shook the place we were staying and I ran out with the others to look for what obviously was a one hundred strong band of drums. It wasn't and this enormous sound was coming from a small group of locals strumming their snare and banging their bass. It was so loud and they marched past the albergue, turned and marched past us again. Someone asked if they were practicing for something and someone suggested that they may be closing off the party that had been going on earlier. Two words came to my mind "Wicker Man" I said, I think it's part of a ritual and we are the .........(if you have watched the movie then you know what I mean) The others laughed, nervously, and we made our way back inside with the drums of the band fading into the darkness of this sleepy town. After I went to bed and I just could not get to sleep. I think I may have been too warm and my thoughts were racing a bit. I remember it was after one and I was putting on go-to-sleep relaxing music.

I woke up and I felt tired and probably was actually a wee bit grumpy (in a tired kind of way) and just stayed out of the way and didn't say much till after breakfast. I set off before the others and it didn't take long, seconds maybe, until the Camino wrapped its warm arms around me and the soothing feeling of the crisp air had me inhaling deep breaths of happiness and I paused to just take it in. I had enjoyed the hospitality of Azofra and especially the kindness of Angel. The Way opened up its path and I was heading for Granon.

The Camino has a unique ability to change its scenery by turning a corner and the endless rows of vineyards started to retreat and give way to the advancing green grass and flowing hills. Walking along looking at all this greenery was amazing and I thought to myself that I'd never seen so many shades of green in one place. I came to a T junction and there were arrows drawn into the dirt pointing one way and an arrow made of stones pointing the other way. My guide was out and I deduced that going right was the correct option so I scribed a message for my fellow Pellegrino's to ensure they knew what way to go and that the message was true. It read "King of Scotland Iain" with an arrow pointing the correct way. My friends followed and soon I saw them with all the college students a km or so back. I waited as this was the most amount of people I had seen on the Camino at one time. I was not to know that this was nothing to what was coming later.

Moving on and climbing more I seen a distinctive green in the distance. The green was the kind that little white balls go on. A golf course and the town of Ciruena. Entering the town, I remembered from reading somewhere that the golf club welcomed in Pellegrino's and as I had not had breakfast or coffee this was the place. I waited for the others to come into town and we all stopped in "the golfy" for hot coffee, tortilla and pastries. It was delicious and I savoured every mouthful. We chatted about this and that and Iain the Australian was talking about how golf was invented in Scotland. I just said I told you everything came from Scotland to the others. I've given the group an example of Scottish inventions and discovery every day so today I simply said. "Yes, the iPhone came from Scotland also" They all looked at me and said no way. I said "of course it was first known as the "och aye phone!"" they got the joke and we did laugh.

We left the golf club and had our waterproof gear on as, believe it or not, it had started snowing. Moving through the town we passed the police who were stopping certain roads from being used and people in yellow vests were manning stations. It soon became clear that something was happening and as we headed out of town it all became clear. The Camino was also, for today, the route for the Rioja Marathon. We headed on and it was not long before the lead car sped along the Camino with a rather fast runner behind it. Soon after droves of people started to pass us. I loved this. I could feel the energy of all these people and I thought about when I had been tired and a simple "Buen Camino" from a stranger would give me energy and a good feeling. I stopped often to bang my poles together in applause and shout encouragement to these determined souls. Often their head would lift and a smile come across their face. Some with a thumbs up and many with a shout of "Buen Camino" ensured both runners and this walker danced into the historic town of Santo Domingo. I was in a very happy place.

Entering Santo Domingo, we were heading for the cathedral. The burial place of the St Dominic. There was a great story told to me that they keep a cockerel and hen there. I asked why? The story goes that a young pilgrim stayed at an albergue with his parents. The owner's daughter wanted to sleep with him and he said no. She was upset so placed a piece of the owner's silver in the boy's belongings and he was convicted of stealing the item and was sentenced to hang by the neck which he did. The parents had plead to St Dominic to save their son and the Saint said that he was not dead. The parents went to the "sheriff

" to say their son was not dead. He was just about to eat and there were two chickens on his plate. The sheriff laughed and said that their son was as alive as the two chickens on his plate. At that moment, the two birds jumped up and danced. Their son was alive.

The cathedral is beautiful and the Saint is buried there. Relics also survive and can be seen. I took some time to look around this spectacular building and think of the millions of pilgrims who have walked on those very stone floors. We ate lunch which I washed down with a rather delightful non-alcohol beer and we were off again. All at our own pace and with my belly happy and my feet extremely happy.

The final walk of the day was again beautiful. The green hills were again showing their colour. I listened to my music and discovered that I am taking the words in more. I'm listening better. Soon I was way ahead and I stopped at a clearing where there was a concrete seat. I took my rucksack off and put it on the slab, lay on it and let the Spanish sun meander its way through some clouds and trees onto my very welcoming face. I couldn't help but lie there in the middle of a Spanish field on a concrete block and think that this was beautiful. It was pure relaxation and I didn't think of anything other than the sun, clouds and tree branches.

Rising, and with my gear back, on I headed into the town of Granon where we were planning on staying the night. I was waiting for others to catch up and as they approached me through the dead street a kid let off a firecracker which sounded like a loud gunshot. As I looked at the others, I fell to the ground as if I'd been shot. They looked at me like I was some sort of idiot and laughed. I was rolling about laughing. Nothing better than laughing at your own jokes.

We found the albergue which works on a donation basis and my mind was just about to be blown more than I could imagine. It's located in the church that was part of an old monastery. Heading through a small door and up the narrow stone steps we were met by a friendly volunteer who welcomed us into the warmest homely place I'd been. Then I noticed the donation box. I read it and looked at the money inside and I knew I was in a kind and loving place. The inscription on the donation box that's sitting wide open reads "Give what you can or take what you need." Incredible, just incredible. Oh, and it gets better. The man introduces us to Oliver the German who volunteers also and we are shown to the loft that overlooks the living area. No bunk beds here. This is pilgrim central where they work on donations so a mat and floor space is provided. My space looked over the community area where you have dinner. So, what is for dinner I thought. I was then told that dinner was being cooked for all of us and breakfast is also provided in this donation only place. Then we ate. Cooked and provided by the people who run this albergue for people. It was a beautiful stew with meat and one without for vegetarians and then desert.

The volunteers ate with us and before dinner we all held hands and he prayed and I sure said thanks for what was happening. The volunteers then sang before we ate. It was sensational. We ate and laughed and the wine flowed and we got talking to our new Pellegrino friends who had joined us. Thomas and his friend from Sweden, a guy from France and, of course Jen, from North Carolina. I first heard Jen when I was sitting up the stairs on my mat and I heard her saying she was from the United States to someone. I then seen her and she said to the other Iain(Australia) "are you Iain?" He said "yes". She said, "Iain from Scotland?" He said "no". I'm now looking down "I'm Iain from Scotland" with an additional "my reputation obviously precedes me!" She replied, "hey I'm Jen from the US." Still wondering how she has heard of me she told me that she had met Luise who had told her about our group. Jen then asked if I was cycling as she had heard about an Iain from Scotland who was cycling The Camino in the previous town and that she had seen the King of Scotland I'd written on the Camino. My name is making its way out into the Camino which made me chuckle.

After dinner, as if today couldn't spring any more surprises it did. Our hosts had a tour with history ready for us. We all went to a room where we were told the history of the church and monastery. They told us how the villagers were grateful and wanted to always help pilgrims. They all contributed to keep the albergue open and running. The phrase used was this

"Some give with money, some give with hand". I thought that was beautiful and they led us into the darkened candle lit area of the church where the monks sat over five hundred years ago on the very seats we were now on. There was a ceremony where a candle was passed around and we all said something to ourselves as we held it. It was an immensely powerful and emotional moment for me. We stood and held hands in a circle and some words were said in Spanish. The village does not give you a stamp for your pilgrim passport. They ask that you hug each other and wish the other person well on "The Way" and that's just what we all did. Words cannot describe exactly the emotions I feel. They are great ones, that I know. Everyday something amazing happens on The Way. I see something, learn something and meet someone new. Ten days in and I wonder what the next twenty something hold. I'll just live them as they happen.

Buen Camino.

"This is your life.
Do what you want and do it often.
If you don't like something, change it.
If you don't like your job, quit.
If you don't have enough time, stop watching TV.
If you are looking for the love of your life, stop; they will be waiting for you when you start doing things you love.
Stop over-analysing, life is simple.
All emotions are beautiful.
When you eat, appreciate every last bite.
Life is simple.
Open your heart, mind and arms to new things and people, we are united in our differences.
Ask the next person you see what their passion is and share your inspiring dream with them.
Travel often; getting lost will help you find yourself.
Some opportunities only come once, seize them.
Life is about the people you meet and the things you create with them, so go out and start creating.
Life is short, live your dream and wear your passion."
~ Holstee Manifesto

# Day 11

## My mind likes to talk
## Granon to Villambistia

Last night finished with the priest, theologian, Luise and myself sitting in the darkened living room area. Luise wrote her diary and I sketched her doing that. It was very relaxing and I thought about what creativity must have been about when you had no gadgets to watch or play with. I fear there are millions of artists, poets, writers, musicians and other creative minds out there that are not being used to their potential as they may not know.

I headed to my mat to sleep and Luise was next to me and then Tiger next to her. All three squeezed in a space for three sleeping bags. Another thing you just have to get used to in some places on the Camino. I remember thinking I really need to do this with Cameron Diaz. It was a bit of a rough night sleep wise. I kept getting a sharp pain through my foot every so often, I got twitchy legs and I seemed to get an itch here and there all the time. I downloaded an app, played relaxation music, read but it was still near 3am before I dozed off.

Everyone was up sharpish and I lay there thinking do not be grumpy. I was fine but a little tired and I went down and joined everyone for breakfast which was great and there was muesli, coffee, bread and jam. A feast indeed. I had already decided that I was going to walk slowly today. It was around the usual 23 km walk to our next destination of Villambistia. The choice of this town was that it was about the distance we usually walk and the albergues in the towns either side were closed. The list we had received had been wrong a couple of times but we have something better than a guide. We have an Alexandro. A Dr of theology but also a fluent Spanish speaker that can phone places in advance. Everyone should take an Alexandro with them if going on the Camino.

I watched as the others headed away up the town and into the distance and I put my music on and started the day's walk. The quiet street of Granon opened up into green rolling fields. This would be the scenery for all of the day. Not long out of the village saw me cross the regional line from La Rioja into the region of Castilla y Leon. This region is the one I believe we will be in for the next 400 or so kms.

The scenery was not unlike the east coast of Fife region back home with lots of small farms and farming communities dotted along the way. As I walked along to the left were snow covered hills and to the right the main N-120 road. At one point I was looking at the snow and then to the right looking at the first ever Spanish snow plough I'd ever seen. I never knew they existed. Every day is a school day and I thought please do not let it snow.

More green fields led to more and more green fields and I passed through the rural villages of Redecilla del Camino and Castildelgado which were quiet and showing signs of attention required. I liked them though as it was no frills farming Spain to me.

During my walk I was very aware at how my mind was trying to do it's make up stories and solve issues that were not even there. Had I been "over joking" with people on the Camino? Had I insulted anyone and before I knew it I had made up scenarios in my head. I thought I'll just go with these thoughts and see where my brain takes me. Arriving in my own stupidville I had to tell me brain to stop worrying. My experiment on myself was an interesting bit of time and you can really let your imagination take over and come up with really crazy scenarios if you let it get away. It was time for a coffee.

I stopped into an albergue and the others were there. It was a cool little rustic place that with a donation you got coffee, bread and a hard-boiled egg along with a well-earned rest. The chat was good and as usual we all headed off at different times on our own towards the large town of Belorado.

More kms and nothing but green rolling hills and my mind was darting back and forth to some really not interesting things. I was worrying about silly things like jobs, debt, clearing of debt, lack of love, where I am in life, single, fitness, health, divorced, not seeing my son and again love. Wait I thought. This is the Camino and I was guessing my mind was using the beautiful relaxing scenery to pop a few questions out there but this time no crazy solutions. This was becoming real me time. Get used to this Iain I thought.

Entering the town of Belorado it was time to eat and I stopped at the first bar and found our two Swedish friends, Jen the girl from the U.S. and Tiger the priest. Warm welcomes were exchanged and tortillas were ordered, then another and then a sandwich. I love this tapas lunch thing and Jen showed me pictures of the application trail in the US that she has done. Very impressive and maybe I need to think about that next. It's about 2000 odd miles.

After lunch, I looked at my emptyish wallet and thought I'd better pick up some euros from the auto bank. My budget was slightly out for the first 10 days and I put that down to the fact that Coca Cola is about 5 times more expensive than wine. There downing wine for pennies and I'm addicted to Coca Cola. A more expensive addiction in these parts. Not to worry though as I had said to all the group that as the donation box at the last albergue also said take what you need that I took all the donations they put in so the five-star hotel would be nice. I'm joking of course I said to them. I think my donation was a generous one for the previous night's stay with food. I went to the bank and withdrew some euros and thought I'd see how far they got me. Leaving the town there was, as always, some cool graffiti and again the town was soon behind me and green fields were my companions again. It was 8km to our place of stay and after what seemed five minutes I was in the very farming village of Tosantos and I knew that my place was only 2km on. Carved into the rock on the cliffs that stand above the town of Tosantos is the Our lady of the Crag or Ermita de la Virgen de la Pena (la Chiesa) which had a 12th century image of the Christ child. Someone said it is always locked so I just took a picture.

Arriving in Villambistia I found the albergue which is the only one in town and treated myself to a non-alcohol beer which I ordered in fluent Spanish. Who'd have thought. The place is nice and soon everyone was there. Time for dinner. I had left a couple of KOS markers in the path as I find it amusing and many of the group now just call me King of Scotland. If only they knew that it really is true.

After a most fantastic shower we headed down for dinner. Remembering we are in a town with a population of around fifty and there are twelve staying, all I can say is we were treated like kings. The stay for our bed, breakfast and our three-course homemade dinner with four bottles of wine and Coke for me was ridiculously cheap at €15 each. The woman who runs the albergue could not do enough. I'm glad we have gone away from the guidebook stages and are stopping at places in between. People are blowing my mind by the day. I will go and paint with a heavy belly, full heart and content mind.

> *"If you wish to be a warrior prepare to get broken, if you wish to be an explorer prepare to get lost and if you wish to be a lover prepare to be both."~ Daniel Saint*

*A cross on the way*

# Day 12
## The Brits are here
## Villambistia to Atapuerca

After such an amazing dinner, I grabbed my paints and sat in the little bar of the albergue ready to paint anything from the day through, what were now, quite heavy eyes. I painted a well I'd seen that day. A well where many dreams had been wished for. I never wished at it as those dreams and wishes I have are alive within me. I could hear the well whisper keep moving Iain. Your dream is ahead.

Once I had finished, I was packing up my paints when the owner woman of the albergue came and sat down. A couple of the others were there also and she wanted to see my paintings from every day. She was great and critiqued everyone in a way that if it was a city picture then she didn't want to know but if it was the country she would write the name of the place on the back. She asked if I would send her a painting and I will have to try and remember to do that. Inmaculada had been another amazing host. A Spanish woman with passion and she ran the place with efficiency and love. After this I headed to bed where the energy in the dorm room was great. I was holding court as usual and there was great banter all round. When I was changing for bed one of the girls said oh you've got more tattoos. I got into bed saying yes (the twelve people in the dorm are all listening to this) I said I also have the letters KOS tattooed on my "little man". She said "really!". I said "yes". She asked why. I said because when I'm "happy" it reads King of Scotland. I swear the theologian and future priest were laughing so hard and when the joke was explained to the others so did they. We all then went to sleep with laughter in our thoughts.

Tiger, the future priest, had hidden my guide book thinking it was fun the evening before so in the morning when I got up I was playing childish jokes on Tiger. I put a copy of the book Zohar in his sleeping bag, then again in his rucksack and he laughed every time he found it. All so I could get a picture of him holding it and I could then arrange the pictures as if he was nicking it. Silly fun but it got the day started.

We ate breakfast which consisted of a muffin and microwave hot water and instant coffee and set off towards our new place of Atapuerca which was around 23 km away. Well all of us apart from Iain and Trish the Australians as Iain had left his jacket in the bar and it had been stored for security and the lady would not be there till later.

We headed along the Camino through the greenery again and the small village of Espinosa del Camino with its colourful houses and I caught up with Alexandro and Elea. I wanted to ask our resident theologian a couple of questions. One was about exorcism of the stance of church and is it still done?

Well it is still done and there is a course for priests that they can go on in Rome. A very interesting talk about this and other subjects along with the current political positions of the U.S. and this all ended with an explanation of the Year of Mercy. Alexandro is a tremendous guy and a few km passed as we chatted. We passed the ruin of an old monastery, San Felices, which was cool and before we knew it we were in the village of Villafranca Montes de Oca and it was proper breakfast time. Tortilla was delicious as was the coffee. It was a busy wee place and was the Spanish version of a truck stop I think.

Lunch finished I headed away first through the busy village traffic wise and took the steep hill up past the church. It was the first big hill in while and my calves were feeling it. About ten minutes into my accent I came upon writing in the ground and I laughed as I could not figure it out. The whole group was behind me but there quite clearly in the middle of The Way were the letters "KOS." The King of Scotland reputation was now ahead of me and travelling fast across the Camino. The trek up the hill towards the summit of around 2500ft was nice as the landscape changed and trees were either side of the path and the remains of the previous snowfall was now showing. The air was getting colder and that along with the heat of my body and the opening views was a great feeling. Continuing along the summit and the plateau there were various bits of art in the form of tree carving and stones in shapes and phrases. There was one shaped as a heart and I got down and painted a message on one. A symbol of love and friendship. I love that kind of stuff as it comes right from my most inner thoughts and feelings.

Luise and Tiger had caught up with me here and we shared some chocolate and it was at this point that three Pellegrino's walked past. I offered them chocolate and they said no. There accent was clear and I had said hello to the first British people I'd met since I had left. I would later find out their names are Tim, Steph and Becky.

We headed towards the next village and I walked with Luise. I was asking about her home town of Potsdam. The next few km I found incredibly interesting. I assumed that Luise and her family were from West Germany and I asked what it was like when the wall came down. She explained that she couldn't remember as she was only about two years old but her mum was excited and nervous at the thought of the west being open. I stopped and said, "wait you were living in East Germany?" She said yes and I was kind of blown away that I was walking with someone who had lived in East Germany and whose family were from there. Luise told me some amazing stories and one that stood out was of her stepfather who was one day in Berlin and wanted a toy gun. The grandfather said to him he could get it the next day. Her stepfather never got that toy gun as overnight the wall had gone up. I remember watching the Berlin Wall coming down on the TV and it was such a huge event in history and here I was listening to first-hand accounts and stories. It was amazing. Oh, and it started snowing.

We reached the next stop of San Juan de Ortega and the monastery was extremely interesting. I read a bit about the history of the nobility and noticed the links to Scotland and it mentioned the St Andrew's cross as it is held by angels on the crypt. Oh, and there is St John's tomb just sitting there. A beautiful and interesting place before a bite to eat next door. Eating in a local tavern I ordered a tortilla which was dearer than usual and it was made to order. It came out and it was huge. An omelette inside half a French loaf. I dived in and three of us shared.

It was in here I introduced myself to the three Brits who it turns out are on a ten-day walking holiday. Really nice people who were full of energy and this was their first day. We swapped a few stories and they were off as they were staying at the village before us. It was nice to meet some Brits I thought.

Leaving, we set off on our own again for our village for the night. Just before the beautiful village of Ages I caught up with the Brits and they made the decision to walk the final 2.6k to the place we were all staying. Tim and I chatted and he had lots of questions about feet and other Camino walking type things and I laughed at myself as I gave good advice back as if I was a Camino expert. Eleven days in and it's amazing what you learn very quickly. Still lots and lots to learn I imagine.

We all checked into the albergue which was €8 and headed to the local bar for tapas as an appetiser and a non-alcohol beer before it was time to head back as chef Iain was again cooking and this time I fed ten people. Good deed number three of the day complete. It's important to me I give or do something daily that gives some sort of happiness to someone or everyone. It's part of my Camino for me.

There has been many laughs and interesting stories today. The group has expanded again by a few and another great day walking the Camino. I wish I could send just a taste of this experience to the world.

> "Man surprised me most about humanity.
> Because he sacrifices his health in order to make money.
> Then he sacrifices money to recuperate his health.
> And then he is so anxious about the future
> that he does not enjoy the present;
> the result being that he does not live in the present or the future;
> he lives as if he is never going to die,
> and then dies having never really lived." ~ Dalai Lama

# Day 13
## Snow way did that just happen
## Atapuerca to Burgos

The evening had been a success and as others slipped off to their bed I found myself sitting at the table in the kitchen sketching the monastery we had passed that day. My mind was racing and out of the blue an idea for a movie came to my head. As I sketched I became fearful of how true the movie could be but what a great plot and twist. It will be a tremendous read/watch one day. I could write the plot but that thickens as I develop the characters. On going to bed I knew I wasn't going to get to sleep quickly as my mind raced and my legs twitched in unison to my thoughts. You'd have thought I was running the grand national. It's amazing where your head can go when you're in a room full of people and you can't make noise. Eventually I must have fallen into a deep sleep around 2am.

I awoke as the others were packing their bags. A couple had said they might stay two nights in Burgos and me being me I thought I hope I haven't done their heads in. This thought bothered me for the first few kms. I worked my way through it though and again learned more lessons about my brain that likes to head off into the sunset thinking it is El Cid.

Everyone had left and I was the last to head out with my rain gear on as it had been reported that it was raining. To my surprise there was no rain. It was snowing. Heading out of town I couldn't help but think do not get lost, do not go around in circles and seriously why is it snowing again. Climbing the steep climb out of the village it was getting heavy and within a few kms it was getting hard to navigate when I saw some of our group. We talked about how easy it would be to get lost and we set of anyway to where I could see an arrow. The previous thoughts about this and that kept the thoughts of how cold it was away. I walked out in front and I knew it was about 5k to the next village and coffee and tortilla was required. When I arrived at the bar the Australians and Brits were already there and finishing their coffee and soon the Mexican, German and Korean arrived and for some it was brandy time, to heat them up, I was told.

Leaving the village of Cardenuela Riopico the snow had stopped and I took a bit of time to call home and get an update from pops of what was going on and it's always nice to hear a voice from home. It lifts your spirits even more, I thought. I read a message I had received from a friend and she is doing some brave stuff just now so conversed back and forward a couple of messages and my spirits were raised more. So much so I had walked right past the route I wanted to take into Burgos. I knew I could get this way also so kept walking and my thoughts were with my brave friend and I daydreamed a lot.

Life was good and I crossed over the railway tracks into the outer limits of the city. Some people may not like the city but there is something nice about walking into one when you're on the Camino. It gives me energy and I stride along the paved streets as if I lived there all my life. Burgos was my town to share with the world. What I don't understand is why I think that it's quite acceptable to sing loudly and play the drums with my walking poles as the music blares in my ears when I walk anywhere on the Camino. This was proved again today as I sang and drummed my way through the busy shopping areas and old district. I thought if I see a guy in Glasgow doing what I'm doing I'd think he'd lost the plot. Now when I see a guy like that singing I'll just think he is in a good place. Luise had caught up with me at a coffee stop on entering the city and we both walked through the city listening to our own music. We passed through street after street of high rise apartments with every type of shop a city offers. I found myself taking in the shop windows and their styles of display as if it were the first time I had seen such a thing. Like magic you pass from the modern part of town into the historic old part and as I passed a ruined church I noted it had a modern roof and that it was an art Gallery. The building was stunning and I loved the fact that they had used this ruin as a place to show art and it is the entrance to a municipal gallery. I took my hat off and took time to wander round this beautifully amazing place. Leaving this place with a sense of amazement at how they had transformed it into an area that took you right out of the hustle and bustle and transported you to a place of thought and art through an old ruined door.

We were soon in the albergue and by the power of something I cannot explain we, as normal, all arrived within minutes of each other. The municipal albergue is nice and I headed out to see the cathedral. Alexandro told me the story El Cid and I was soon inside this magnificent structure where El Cid himself lies in his resting place. The inside is so immense and has so many chapels that I made the comment that it is possibly just too much to take in. As I stood over El Cid I received a text. It was an invitation and one that I could not turn down. I said goodbye to El Cid, my fellow Pellegrino's and the beautiful building. I was now heading somewhere more important and that was vital to the rest of the Camino now that Id received this text from a number that had never been on my phone before. The excitement was flowing through me as my flip flops skimmed the edge of the five-hundred-year-old steps and my walk was more of a run. I moved across the main square and there was the contact. People that would show me to the place that meant so much to millions of pilgrims but alas only a very special few ever got to experience this. With my secret contact we entered the building that held this shrine and sneaked past the stern looking person manning the security/reception desk. Pressing the elevator button quickly the doors closed and it sped upwards towards heaven. A couple of locked doors and there it was. Sitting proudly, yet as if it was used to the few pilgrims that were lucky enough to experience its charm while walking the Camino. It was the golden bath.

As I listened to the purified water splash the hull of this perfectly designed bath tub my feet sang hymns of joy while my entire body shook in excitement at the thought of the bubbles that were exploding in happy giggles encouraging me to slide in and the feeling of nirvana flowed over every inch of my body. Life was amazing. I had managed to get strangers a day or so before to give me access to their bath and have them to take a photo of me in it. I laughed and laughed at the situation as I lay in the luxury setting thinking of my fellow Pellegrino's. Santiago was looking after me in the most amazing way. I loved my bath and vowed to have more of them in my life.

Floating out of the fancy hotel and I treated my host to a glass of wine and for me a non-alcohol beer that I love. Heading back to the albergue I met the gang heading out for dinner and as we walked through the beautiful city I told tales of soapy bubble baths. Eventually we all finished up in a pizza place and the laughter and talk soon ebbed away into silence as we all tackled the most delicious pizza.

*"If you wish to be a warrior prepare to get broken, if you wish to be an explorer prepare to get lost and if you wish to be a lover prepare to be both." ~ Daniel Saint*

# Day 14

## When people are hungry
## Burgos to Hornillos del Camino

The lights in the albergue were switched off at 10pm and it was off to bed for everyone. The bunks were cool though as they were in their own little cubicle type thing that gave you your own light and power. I decided I'd watch at little bit of Les Misérables laying in my personal comfy cocoon. It wasn't long before my favourite musical had sent me to sleep and it cost me another phone call to Vodafone as while I dreamed a dream my data was draining and draining. Not something I'm worried about as it's all part of this experience.

As we left the albergue we all had one thing to do. Get to a cafe. So, through the driving snow we crossed the street and walked the ten meters to the cafe where we drank coffee and ate tortilla. I then realised I had also left my watch in the albergue when in the cafe and went back to find it under my pillow. I felt relieved that it was there.

Here the group said our farewells to our German friend Luise who had decided to stay and rest for a day. I was a bit sad if I am honest as Luise was full of energy and fun. She had been there from day one and we all had shared some amazing times with her. As I hugged her goodbye I wished her all the best and in my mind, I prayed that her life gave her everything she truly deserved. I hope one day our paths cross again. Buen Camino Luise.

With a warm heart and a full belly, we headed off for the 21km walk to Hornillos del Camino. The snow was heavy and wet and soon we were all laughing at it being our fourth snow day. It must be some sort of record I commented however I know that we were all secretly loving the fact that it was another day of the unexpected. As we navigated our way out of Burgos I realised due to my cold ears that I had left my woollen LOVE hat back in the albergue. I loved that hat I thought.

Alexandro was walking with me and I had already said I had lots of questions for him. Alex never ceases to surprise me with his insane knowledge. While I had been talking to him the previous night I discovered that he did not only study Catholicism but all religions. I had some serious questions for him and he didn't disappoint with his knowledge. Have you read the bible Alex? "yes, when I was twelve". What is the Muslim religion all about and the differences with Christianity. That was an amazing conversation and it was not the differences that surprised me it was the parts that were similar or the same that surprised me. Too much to write down but interesting. Have you read the Koran I asked? Alex reply was "yes, when I was fourteen". He read The Zohar when he was twenty and many of the Buddhist books. Seemingly there are a lot and then I got a brief explanation on Hinduism. It was an amazing lesson again and the kms passed under my feet without even realising and the snow was failing in its attempt to dampen our spirits.

Leaving Alex, I headed forward and caught up with Thomas a fifty-nine-year-old Swedish guy who has a great zest for life and like everyone on the Camino he has his reasons for the walk and we both talked openly and honestly. The Camino I think gives those who walk it the lesson that it's good to talk and it's good to listen. People are amazing I thought.

Reaching the town of Tardajos I was completely surprised as I thought it was the town before. This was the 10km mark and I thought that we had only been walking for a short time. Amazing how two different people and great conversation makes the time fly by. We stopped in a cafe and we were in heaven as the hot coffee was poured and the homemade tortilla was a very welcomed treat. The girl who served us was like an angel sent to warm the hearts of the cold pilgrims with her cheeky smile, encouraging words and her magnetic friendliness. If there was a single Pellegrino not infected by her energy I'd be surprised. She was cute also. The Brits arrived and it was funny as we talked about the snow. With the pace we were going we decided to wait in the cafe and drink more coffee as it was snowing outside.

Our waterproofs back on we headed out into the now non-snowing day that had only light drizzle and cold. I put my earphones in and passed a small church I liked and through the next village of Rabe de las Calzadas and climbed upward towards the plateau and the sunshine I could see waving at me. As I climbed the sun did have its hat on and it was holding it on tight as its friend the wind gained in strength. It was cold but it was beautiful. All this as Justin Beiber came dancing through my earphones. Justin you're OK right now I laughed then I sang along with him.

It's always a great feeling as you catch sight of the place you're staying and I strode downwards and onto the village of Hornillos del Camino where we were staying for the night. The albergue was still closed and we sat in the sun until it was opened. I found my bed and as I unpacked I could not help but shiver as my breath made smoke type clouds in the cold air of the room. It was freezing. I paid my money and as there was no shop or restaurant in the village, with a population of sixty, the guy who runs the albergue sells pasta and such. I decided then I'd cook for everyone. We all put in a couple of euros and I was ready to cook up a storm. As I looked at the table and the others who were staying in the albergue I saw they had all purchased the same things and there was one cooker. The wine was opened and I asked them all to relax as I set to work preparing dinner for the whole albergue of 13 people. I loved cooking and listening to all these new people get to know each other. I get a good feeling like I'm giving something back to the Camino by doing stuff. Another pilgrim arrived and there was a bowl of pasta for him. A German guy who could not be more pleased and appreciative. Then three Italians arrived. They too had some of my delicious pasta and laughing to myself I thought I bet they think I'm Italian with the quality of that pasta dish. Well they ate it and thanked me. All in all, I fed seventeen people and watched as they drank eight bottles of wine. They talked, sang and laughed. New people meeting new people and connecting. Great to watch.

I returned to my room and grabbed my shower things and I was soon in a lukewarm shower scared to get out into the Arctic feeling of the room. I shivered as I dried myself and pulled on anything that was dry. Thomas came in and said, "I'm moving to the next room as it's warmer". Like a couple of school kids, we were carrying our sleeping bags and belongings stealthily into the other room where there were two bunks left. I claimed it and was happy at even a degree warmer. I was happy though and even had a surprise call from Junie my pal. It's nice to hear a voice from home.

A day of emotions and thinking, a day of extreme opposite weathers and a day of new people. We will die and that's a fact so live as much as I can. That's what I'm doing I thought and it feels good.

"One day it just clicks...
you realize what's important and what isn't.
You learn to care less about what other people think of
you and more about what you think of yourself.
You realize how far you've come and you remember when you
thought things were such a mess that you would never recover.
And you smile.
You smile because you are truly proud of yourself and
the person you've fought to become." ~ Unknown

*The amazing Alexandro*

# Day 15

## You should flirt when you get the chance
## Hornillos del Camino to Castrojeriz

The end of the night had come and once again I was on my own in the kitchen area painting. The log fire gave off a welcoming heat and mischievous glow that said I know upstairs is cold. Eventually I headed to my top bunk. The first time I have been on the top one this whole experience. As I slipped into my sleeping bag I noticed that the room was warmer than I thought it would be. I checked some messages unaware of the horror that was about to take place.

It started with one of my friends starting to snore. Not just a little snort but a full on guttural snore. My eyes went wide with shock and immediately I thought thank goodness, I have put my earplugs in a safe place under my pillow. As I was awake I continued to check my email when another and then another and then yet another pilgrim joined in on this chorus of sleeping sounds I never thought was possible. The choir, now four strong, harmonised their snores in an even more emotionally annoying way than I thought possible. I swung round tired and in the dark swiftly felt under my pillow for the lifesaving earplugs. In slow motion I felt the tips of my fingers force the earplugs, that were wrapped up in their secure case, out from the back of the pillow and down into the dark abyss of the rear of the bunk beds. The case played the last post as I heard it clatter to the ground beneath the double bunk bed combination I was sleeping on. They were gone. Earphones in I tossed and turned in rhythm with the choir of the Camino and the next thing I knew the lights were on and time to get up. I jumped out of bed and was ready to go. Cheap coffee and supermarket already toasted bread we set off for our 20km trip to Castrojeriz.

The weather threatened to rain and I realised that I had left my poncho in the albergue and I went back to find it locked. Two days in a row I had left something. The thing that eased this pain was that Luise had messaged me to say that she had recovered my blue LOVE hat that I had left the previous day. The Camino gods required their sacrifice and I was now happy to give them the poncho as the hat was far more important. We climbed out of the town and the priest, the theologian and the last king of Scotland entered their morning theological conversation with questions always posed by myself. What is purgatory? Why is Moses important? What is hell and how's it defined by the church? What makes Protestantism different from Catholicism? Tell me what you know about Martin Luther? As we passed on to the plateau we talked and debated and I asked and asked more questions and I loved the answers as it was interesting. Alexandro is a fountain of knowledge and facts and Tiger, the going to be priest, is passionate about his faith.

Social agendas and economic policy thrown into the mix and the kms again passed and the blue skies broke through, lighting up the horizon that was now visible.

Tiger and I moved on as Alex waited for his wife and for a few kms the priest and I talked of love, what that meant and how that felt for each of us. Had he loved and how did that affect a young man now in the seminary. I told him my views and told him a story of love and we talked and talked. A conversation that I will remember for a long time. The priest that opened up to the me and my thoughts were of love. I smiled and we moved down into a small village of Hontanas for lunch. A beautiful morning of conversation.

The team were there along with my new British friends. Tim who had drank a few last night is a true gentleman and has a wicked sense of humour and a guy you could just sit and listen to. We all ate and I was soon on my way alone. It was that time of day and my thoughts were dancing around at the start line ready to race forward to see who could win the time on that afternoon's Camino. As usual many of them had their few minutes as I contemplated life, love and the beauty of the nature that was wrapping itself around me as I walked. I remember thinking to myself that I was just content at that moment. I passed by the monastery of St Anton where they attended to pilgrims as far back at the twelfth century. It was amazing to walk through the arch and know that hundreds of thousands of pilgrims for many centuries had passed through this very spot.

Soon the town of Castrojeriz was in view with its magnificent fortress on top of the hill. The churches dominated the skyline and I walked along the tree lined road into the town. My stride was quick and as I entered the town an old man in a van held out a stamp for my Compostela. He had wooden trinkets in various shapes in a large jar and after giving me a stamp he pointed at the euro coin on a piece of paper and the jar of wooden trinkets. Remembering that I had read about pilgrims buying trinkets when I was visiting the historic town of St Andrews back home I passed over my Euro coin. He opened his jar of wooden carved crosses and right at the top was a wooden heart, as if to say I'm here I've been waiting for you. This was indeed a good omen and I thanked the old man for the heart. This was now my Camino Heart and I knew exactly where it would eventually go and to whom. Walking through the quiet but stunning town I soon found the albergue and when I walked in I was greeted with the amazing Eduardo. It was so great to catch up with one of the pilgrims who started with us. Eduardo is the quirky Italian who had forgotten his clothes in day one. We embraced and laughed and headed out to catch up with a non-alcohol beer for me and as we sat in the sun with the chilly air in a town that sits around 1900ft the day had been good.

I entered the shower with a keen sense of excitement as it had been reported that they were fantastic. I was not disappointed and the warm solar heated water soothed and cleaned my welcoming skin. It was bliss. I came out and lay on my bunk which seemed to wrap itself around me and for the first time this trip I slipped into a well-earned and needed afternoon nap.

I awoke and the room was empty. My nap had been bliss and I headed out of the albergue to catch up with my new friends at the local bar. A great bunch of people. I sat and wrote this while listening to Tim and Alex debate a whole bunch of subjects. I told Steph (the vet from London) that I had spotted her sexy legs as she came from the shower and we all laughed. A group of people who days ago were on their own journey and who now are sharing a special experience with new friends. Life just keeps getting better.

> "It's a terrible thing, I think, in life to wait until you're ready.
> I have this feeling now that actually no one is ever ready to do anything.
> There is almost no such thing as ready.
> There is only now. And you may as well do it now.
> Generally speaking, now is as good a time as any." ~ Hugh Laurie

# Day 16

## From emergency to happiness
## Castrojeriz to Fromista

There is always something new happening on the Camino and last night was no different. We had finished some snacks and drinks at a local bar and I headed back to the albergue around nine. I sat and painted a picture and watched as the others returned, some with a glow from the local wine, and headed to the spacious heated dormitory. Elea, Alex and I were chatting in the communal area when our forever fun Italian Eduardo came out saying he thinks he needs to go to hospital. He already had a burst knee and had been sick for the previous day or so. I assumed that was what was wrong and asked what was up. In his own amazing version of broken English, he was peeling up his shirt showing the rash that was literally consuming his body. Another guy joined us and we got Alex to call the emergency number. We had established that Eduardo had eaten nothing else but nuts a short time before and he was now complaining that his breathing was getting harder. After conversations with the operator we were told that an ambulance was on its way. Eduardo's skin was a mess with the rash and the reaction was clearly taking hold. It would take the ambulance around twenty minutes to get out to the albergue. During that time, we woke up Steph who is a vet but has knowledge of medicine obviously. She was great and ensured Eduardo was calm and we held ice against him and then the ambulance arrived. Along with the ambulance came another car with a doctor and another woman so we had 4 medical people, Alex translating, Elea, Tiger, a French guy and myself walking about in the background, the Albergue owner chatting, Steph and, of course, the patient. I sat and watched as everyone played their role. Steph the Vet was hilarious as the Dr gave a steroid injection and said if he fell became sick again we had to drive him to the hospital. Steph replied in Spanish do you want me to take him on my horse. Tiger packed Eduardo's rucksack and fetched Coke, Alex had to go with the albergue guy to a hospital 17 km away to get medicine as the Dr had run out. The French guy went to bed and I took the ever-important task of eating toast and jam while entertaining Eduardo and the rest with silly tales, massaging the vets neck and eating more toast. Everyone eventually went to bed and I volunteered to administer Eduardo's medicine at 4am. I lay in the dark and there was no way I was going to sleep due to being paranoid I'd sleep through my alarm and miss giving the Italian his medicine. Just before 4am Steph passed by my bunk as she couldn't sleep either and we went and fetched Eduardo's meds and woke him up to take them. He was his usual hilarious lovely self. He had been sound asleep and was so grateful that , through sleepy eyes as I placed the tablets in his mouth to take, he was repeating I love you both to Steph and me and wanting to hug. Eduardo had a fright and was exhausted. I think we all were and soon I was sound asleep.

I woke up at 7.30am feeling OK and soon the albergue was talking of the previous night's events and I checked on Eduardo. He was fine and as usual was ready to continue his Camino journey. We laughed and soon he was on his way and I left the albergue happy knowing my Italian friend, who has had one thing after another, was soldiering on. What a guy I smiled. Walking up the narrow streets with the priest, the theologian and Elea we soon left the town of Castrojeriz on our 25 km journey to Fromista.

It looked like The Way was mostly flat today except for a wee hill at the start. The wee hill was a workout and as we strode up it didn't take long for the priest, the theologian and myself to get into some great conversation. I asked them to tell me about the Mass, why is it important, what about this and what about that. As most mornings, I ask endless questions on religion and other topics and Alex and Tiger talk passionately about their views and answers while I fling in questions that come into my head. Are there secret orders in the church, what's the views on Opus D. Explain to me the story of Martin Luther again, what effect did the second world war have on Judaism. Immensely complicated and deep subjects but I had to remember that Alex had his PhD at the age of twenty-one and was a professor of theology. While the subject large and deep it never felt like that and the chats were again so interesting. The top of the hill appeared and the view back and the view forward to where we were going was beautiful. Ahead lay a few hundred kms of flatness. Onward to the next village of Itero de la Vega as it was time for cafe con leche and any type of food available. As I walked I missed my blue LOVE hat as it was cold so I was given a bandanna for my ears. How cool was I as I stepped into a new region for the first time?

We had caught up with Eduardo and the Australians and I had a breakfast of bacon, egg and chips. It was insanely good and again we headed off in search of the next village of Boadilla del Camino. Alex and I talked about many subjects on this 8km stretch including secret societies, conspiracy theories and again the time flew by before stopping for a coffee.

Refreshed I headed out on my own for the final 6km stretch into the town and about half way I ran into the bold Eduardo again who was entertaining Eric, a young American guy who was here to complete the Camino as he had to stop last time due to blisters. We walked into town together and Eric told how his girlfriend and her eighty-four-year-old father were joining him for the last 100km. I thought I hope I meet this eighty-four-year-old. That's an inspiration right there.

Crossing over the old canal into the town of Fromista we soon found the albergue. Into our rooms we went and it was the usual suspects. I spotted a room with only two bunk beds in it and I asked if it was possible to go in. The thought of a snoring free night was very appealing to me and the woman agreed. My private room, although with no heating, was a luxury. Tiger the priest had soon shown interest and immediately claimed squatter's rights. I pulled my sleeping bag up and prepared for an afternoon nap. Soon I was asleep.

I heard familiar voices and my eyes were blinking slowly as I gazed at the shape of someone in my room and a familiar voice was saying hello. I actually thought I am dreaming for a second as I was looking at Luise my German friend we had left in Burgos two days ago. She smiled and I did also. She had my LOVE hat and had caught up with us. The original group was getting back together and we had more people. The Camino working it's strange yet happy magic yet again. Oh, and my blue hat had found me. There is love I thought in this hat. I'll guard it better now.

Everyone headed out as I lay and started my writing. Later I joined them and the meal commenced with some fun as always jokes and talk ensued. My Camino dream gets better by the day. Life is good and thoughts are electric.

## A POEM TO A FUTURE PRIEST

To Tiger a Priest for sure
In search of peace and that one cure
A man who eats just quite a lot
And wears a poncho that he once bought

He laughs and smiles at all things fun
While caring for our future nun
The man that has one dear young sister
But his real pain is his big heel blister

I pray to God for our young Cho
No stripper clubs and no young Ho
Keep up your faith and look above
The answers there about the one you love


"We either make ourselves miserable, or we make ourselves strong.
The amount of work is the same." ~ Carlos Castaneda

# Day 17

## Emotional and beautiful – Nuns rock
## Fromista to Carrion de Los Condes

The night was good and as I settled into my two-bunk luxury private pad that I had managed to worm my way into. Tiger the priest had joined as had my old pal Luise and while it was cold it was nice to be in a place with few people. A little break was needed. After some goodnight John Boy Walton type procedures, the lights went out and I decided to watch a movie that the priest had recommended. It was called Man on Earth. It was OK but I must have fallen asleep during it. I awoke a few times as it was pretty cold and there were no snorers which was good. Well when I say no snorers I was informed by Luise in the morning that I did have a couple of little snores. That was deliberate of course as they had invaded my secret room so I didn't want them to feel as if they were not on the Camino. At another point I woke up and deleted loads of music that I don't even know how it got on my iPhone and then remembered that I had Amazon Prime so downloaded Les Misérables, some of the three tenors and time to say goodbye by Beloci.

Thomas the Swede and I left the albergue in the search of breakfast and coffee. It was chilly and I was so pleased to have my hat back. The albergue was right next the beautiful Iglesia de San Martin XlthC which was consecrated in 1066 the battle of Hastings sprung to mind. Seemingly it is one of the finest examples of pure Romanesque in Spain. I looked at its beauty in awe under the cool but bright blue sky. Many a pilgrim had stood on that very spot and looked at this same church. A good start to the day. We found a bar that was selling beautiful pastry and cake and we were soon up to our eyes in yumminess. The rest of the group arrived and we all ate and drank. Today was going to be an easy day in the grand scheme of things as it was only 19.3km and it was a beautiful morning.

Heading out of town we were in the sleepy village of Poblacion de Campos and within no time the priest, the theologian, the house dragon (our pet name for the Alexando's wife Elea), Thomas and I were all chatting and taking it easy as we chose to take the scenic route out of the town. Luise and a new pilgrim Alex from Brazil passed us and they were heading for a 38km day. As they moved on by us I commented to our group that Alex from Brazil, a strong looking young man had only started two days previously, was possibly not going to make it 38km. He was doing that first few days walk that we were all experts in that says " hi I'm your body and I'm hurting. Please take it easy for a bit." I wondered where I would see them again as they were both great full-of-life people. The way out of town was well marked and we knew that we had lots of time. The conversation was not too deep at all this morning and it was not long before I had sung a couple of verses of Willie McBride and asked what the national anthems of each country represented was. Thomas sang the Swedish, Tiger sang the South Korean anthem, Alex said he could not remember the Mexican tune I didn't believe him but between us we got it and the German anthem gave us a good chat about why many Germans do not sing a nationalistic anthem. Very interesting. I ,of course, sang a few songs including our national anthem. It was fun as our own little version of the Eurovision song contest took place. We were looking for coffee now and the village of Villarmentero de Campos was coming into view. We entered and I sang the Clint Eastwood tune that sounds like an owl – ooooweeeooo ooooweeeooo. We were five gunslingers going into a town that was deserted and ready to take on whoever it was for coffee. The whoever it was turned out to be a lonely dog and a sheep. Not another person or living thing was spotted. We left the town in an even more desperate search for coffee.

It was a straight walk of 4 km to the town of Villacazar de Sigra and we all set off at our own pace. My newly downloaded three tenors and Pavarotti grabbed my ears attention and the horizon stretched out as far as I could see. It was amazing as it sounded like the music was coming from all directions. Walking into town I found the cafe where hot coffee was being served and my fellow pilgrims were there. Carbonara was on the menu. As the woman cooked up a storm I could literally feel my mouth water with anticipation. I wasn't disappointed and with my belly full I headed across the street to visit the village church. This was no ordinary church though. This is the church of Santa Maria. A magnificent Templar church that houses the tombs of nobility and is a now a national monument. Every time I go into a church here I am blown away by its incredible beauty and structure. When I entered I just thought oh my Lord what a place.

Leaving the village for the walk to our finish town the sun was shining and the cool breeze nipped at my cheeks as I entered the land of Les Misérables. I sang and listened to the music and words of what is by far is my favourite theatre show. Probably because I've never been to see another one however I find it hard to think anything could compare. I met the bold Eduardo as we entered the town and I played my Italian friend Nessun Dorma by Pavarotti. Eduardo can always make me smile.

A shower later and I had a nap as at 5pm the nuns were having a sing along and we were all going. Five o'clock came and the nuns came in. Three nuns run the albergue and one came with her guitar. They had been all smiles from the minute we arrived and you could literally feel the love coming from these three amazing women. What happened next was one of the most emotional and powerful times of my life. With smiles they talked through our translator Alexandro. To explain the words they spoke is hard. It is something you have to experience yourself. They sang songs and they were good. We all said where we were from and why we were on the Camino. All these people from all over the world just being honest about why they were there. I'm still finding out why and said I feel like it's a calling to walk the Camino. I'm finding things out every day. Thinking deeper than I've ever thought and been the most content at times than I have ever been. The nuns said sing number three. As we all started singing Amazing Grace I got to the second line and my eyes were filling and by the third line I was indeed in an emotional place and the tears flooded down my face. I was not embarrassed even though I shielded my face. I didn't understand why I was being emotional but I knew it felt like a good emotion and that it was like another part of release. The "I once was lost" part had struck a chord and here I was crying in front of three happy loving nuns. Why? I'm not lost any more.

I looked up and I wasn't the only one and as there were more songs the singing got louder and even though they were in Spanish our Spanish song sheets were being well used. Tiger the priest sang a song from Korea and it was beautiful. A beautiful singer and he surprised us all. The Germans sang a song and at the end the nuns sang a blessing and as they did this one nun came and laid her hands on my head and said a prayer. I was then given a star to symbolise light. I was gone again. As the nun performed this around all the pilgrims there was hardly a dry eye in the house. People just letting their emotions go and it felt good to be part of something that was way bigger than me. Religious or not and some who were also crying are not. It's a moment in my life I will never forget. It was perfect.

I will sleep tonight and I know I'll thank whoever for these three-kind beautiful and loving women who in a short period of time gave me something I hope many others will get to experience.

It's Sunday and as it is a day of rest it was time to go out for dinner so the group all headed out. I was hungry.

> "You can meet somebody tomorrow who has better intentions for you than someone you've known forever... Time means nothing... Character does." ~ Unknown

# Day 18

## A straight road to happiness
## Carrion de Los Condes to Ledigos

I had arrived in bed a happy and tired man with the one problem being that I had mislaid my earphones. I seem to lose something every day and it's become a standing joke within the group. Tiger the priest knew that I had trouble getting to sleep and said I was to use his earphones. A lovely guy and I got in my bunk and started to download Pavarotti's ultimate collection for the open plain that were to come. Talking of plains, I found it amusing trying to teach Tiger that the rain in Spain falls mainly on the plain. Still not got there. Switching on, the forever culture show, Still Game I lay back and within minutes I was asleep.

I awoke to everyone in the room getting on with their packing and I had slept right through except for one bathroom break. I got up, packed and headed out into the chilly but beautiful morning. The little town with the amazing Nuns was quiet and I knew that it held many, many happy emotions as people walked out and onto new places. Stopping of for the normal coffee ritual I ordered a sandwich which I shared with Luise as it was huge. As I still had not found my earphones and I had

Pavarotti on hold I asked Alex to ask the barman if there was a shop open for me to buy some. The answer was not until 10am. I resigned myself to no music for the day however the mislaid headphones had proved a help in another way. When everyone had left, I had looked under the bed I was meant to sleep on (it was a top bunk and I switched to a bottom one) and then under the pillow of the bottom one and there I found a pair of good, clean hiking socks. As I sat and smelled the socks ---I'm joking as that made me laugh. I knew who they belonged to and I ran down the stairs. The Dutch woman was grateful and hugged me for finding her ever important socks. Way more important than earphones so the sacrifice of them to the Camino gods for the socks was worth it. I knew St James would work his magic. It didn't take long and as I was leaving the breakfast bar the barman said to us to wait five minutes as his chica was bringing some headphones from his house to see if they work. They arrived and I asked how much after testing them. He said give me a price so I handed over €5 and was ready for the haggle when he smiled and said gracias. My date with Pavarotti was back on.

The road out of town passed by a beautiful church and a four star hotel that was once a monastery and the place that the British Pellegrino's stayed the night before. It looked beautiful and thought I'd need to give them a hard time when I saw them again for the distinct lack of a phone call to use their bath. I dreamed of having a hotel room when I got to Santiago. The

Way this morning presented zero towns or event habitation for the first 18km so as usual the priest, the theologian and the last king of Scotland set out to talk about whatever came to mind. The subjects varied and we told jokes while listening to each other's retake of the night before. Any subject is accepted in our little United Nations set up. We had said goodbye to Luise and Alex from Brazil yet again at the town as they didn't make the 38km the day before but they were sure they would today.

The road was straight and the horizon stretched as far as I could see in all directions. Some people have called this the boring section of the Camino. I thought how do you get a boring section on the Camino. It's not possible I thought. The view was beautiful and the chat was good. About 10k into the straight road we came upon a tree that sheltered the Brits, Thomas the Swede and Eric the American. They were heading also and we took the obligatory selfie and we all started to head to what we hoped would be a watering hole of sorts.

Steph the Vet and I set the pace and we walked and talked about life in general. Relationships, the stresses of life and we laughed as we are both quite cheeky to each other. I like her and through her tough cheeky exterior I could tell she was a kind person. She was quite good at telling me my obviously amazing jokes were not that amazing. She was wrong of course! We eventually reached the town of Calzadilla de la Cueza and it was time for lunch. The whole gang was there and the chat was flowing and tales of this and that captured people's imaginations. Then a while later and with a laugh and a smile the bold Eduardo arrived.

Fed and watered we set of for the next village of Ledigos. Much discussion had been made about where we were stopping for the night and Eric the American had said his girlfriend had stayed at the La Morena albergue last year and that it was great. I was sold and decided I was staying there and not walking further. We headed towards the town and Steph and I walked ahead and chatted while I told her about Cameron my son and some deep stuff. We passed the old Italian guy who seems to be in many places we stay. He was lying in the grass and shouting hellos in Italian and then I made a KOS mark in the ground for the other Pellegrino's coming behind. It was a lovely walk and in no time, we had reached the town. Ledigos was a great sight and the albergue entrance/bar was modern and lively. The Brits were going to walk on to the next town however after we had checked in and showed them pictures they drank a beer and made the decision to stay. I was happy as the three of them are amazingly funny in their own way and great company. The albergue seemed lovely and it was warm and the chat was good when Brazil Alex and Luise arrived with a German friend. They were in good spirits as they had drunk a few beers in the last town then finished around 3 litres on the walk to here. Everyone sat around and we laughed and solved the world's problems like any group of people does. Life again was good and the

Camino makes the meeting of new people a really enjoyable and important part. I had talked all day and poor Pavarotti had waited patiently. He would have to wait till tomorrow. Brazil and Germany drank more beers then picked up their things to walk/stagger to the next town. There was lots of hugging and goodbyes. Then as usual with a smile and broken English, we welcomed Italy again. As Brazil and Germany staggered off into the evening sun, I predicted that I would soon see them. An hour later they arrived back. I laughed young ones! As dinner approached I decided that the thirty odd minutes I had just stood in the most amazing shower was enough as I was also hungry. Time to eat and learn more about my friends, the Camino and more importantly myself.

Eric the American had said that his girlfriend thought the food was fantastic at the albergue when she stayed before so I headed down with the gang to the dining room where it was only ourselves with a lovely waitress and chef explaining a rather delicious sounding pilgrim menu that was a mere €10 for three courses. I opted for the first course of lentils and chorizo sausage which when it arrived was a meal in itself. I scoffed it down and waited for my second course of meatballs with homemade chips. It was amazing and everyone commented on how great it was. The chat was flowing and as dessert of homemade rice pudding came to say hello I finished off what was the best pilgrim meal I've had so far. Finishing up I quickly left first and settled my bill. I had a date you see. The Brazilian girl was in the next bunk and I had told her I'd be as quick as I can and her smile and broken English of "I'll be right here" had crossed my mind many times during dinner.

I entered the room and she smiled and I dreamed of her hands slowly moving across my body. I smiled back and without words I pulled my top off. She smiled and came closer and motioned for me to take my trousers off and lay on my bed. My heart was thumping as she told me to breath deep and close my eyes. As her hands touched my skin and the electricity from her fingers shot to every extremity of my body I thought to myself........ That's a nice story but the reality was I was just lucky to have a professional masseuse in the next bunk that's doing massages for €10. For the next twenty minutes I let Miss Rio de Awesome work out the aches and pains from my tired body. My calves and feet were in heaven when she completed them. I thought I can see me doing this if I meet her again.

> "Take about your blessings more than you talk about your problems." ~ Unknown

## Day 19

### The Camino dream becomes stronger
### Ledigos to Calzada del Coto

I was tired and off to sleep I went and for an hour or so I slept until I woke up and for the next few hours seemed to have a battle of wits with a new snorer. An Olympian of the sport and as 4am passed I fell asleep through exhaustion. Waking up I was tired, however, I sleepily walked to where everyone was standing and in comedic effect swore often about the snoring and Tim the culprit sheepishly apologised as everyone laughed. My tired mind laughed as I said to everyone "wait I have a poem for Tim" I stood and in true dramatic style I recited the poem of my experience to the group only written hours before.

THE NOISE OF SLEEP


Laying here in my bunk
I heard more snoring
And my heart sunk
It had been all night, With not a rest
I tried to sleep
I tried my best

So, with patience short
And sleep in mind
I thought of ways to be just kind
The nose I pinched
The bed we moved
The snoring stopped
And we were soothed

Then I lay there is disbelief
as again it started
OH good grief
The snoring King
Well he was here
And on my cheek
I felt a tear

Dear sleep I said
Will you be kind

an hour or two
Please help me find
I'm tired and need to rest
Give me a break
from the snoring pest

And then it started
Not one but two
A competition
And I felt blue
This is a joke
What have I done
Why did I not just pack a gun

Depressed and sad
I just give in
And all the earplugs
Went to the bin
A plan was needed
Now just be smart
And then I heard the first loud fart

My eyes shot wide
My nostrils closed
Someone's undies
Now need disposed
Come on this can't be true
To snore and fart

*Then right on Q*

*A compilation*
*Of all above*
*I jumped up and screamed*
*Right that's enough*
*On deaf ears my screams just fell*
*I now I knew*
*That this was hell*

*To my knees, I dropped*
*I began to pray*
*What were the words*
*I had to say*
*Forgive me,*
*show me the light*
*And just like that I went night night.*

To applause and laughs I headed for coffee. The young ones were suitably hungover and through groans of never on the Camino again I smiled and was happy to see them having such a great experience. Tim the snorer kidded on about having a wine. I think he really wanted to. He is a truly funny kind gentleman. Emphasis on the funny.

I headed of on my own and the sun was out however the white crystals of frost blinked in the light that managed to creep through the hedgerows. I took this time to give pops a call and it was good to hear his voice and talk about a little of the experience as I walked along the Camino. There is something special in that and I was excited to update him on some of the things I have done and people I have met.

Soon I caught up with the Brits and passed with a hello. I was in my zone with music playing and thoughts of the Camino in my mind. I couldn't help but think about the great people I had met and how quickly you can bond with people. After a few kms the village of Moratinos came into view and I hoped that there was coffee and food ready for me. The first house was an open cafe and I went in and coffee and tortilla was ordered. The others soon arrived two by two and the ark was soon full of hungry pilgrims ready for their morning break. Fully refreshed it was time for the priest, the theologian, his wife and myself to head off in search of our next stop. The village was interesting though as there was a mound with what looked like tombs. On investigation, it turns out that these five-hundred-year-old entrances are where locals store wine, food and cheese. We would see another one that day as a woman was actually putting her groceries in. No fridges here I thought. The four of us headed and laughed at the Halloween decorations on the walls outside the place we ate. Tiger the priest literally jumped out of his skin when we brought him around the corner saying look at the size of that spider. There was a fake huge spider covering the side of the hotel. I thought it's obviously fake but he really got a fright. I laughed a lot. We walked and soon passed through San Nicolas del Real Camino and on to the border with the next regionLeon. The chat was good and I spent some time with Elea the German wife to Mexican Alexandro. She is also a lovely person who I give a bit of a hard time to every day as I'll deliberately say a number or distance that I know is not correct or just a little out and the German efficiency kicks in to correct me. I'll laugh and so will she. She's also a clever woman and teaches German while living in Mexico. She was telling me how one time she learned Swedish, Finnish and Danish all at the same time for a bit of fun to see the differences. I thought I am happy with saying thank you here in Spain and in English.

We had all caught up and we crossed the Rio Valderaduey where the little church Virgen del Puente sits and two newish beautiful markers show the geographical centre of the Camino. A group photo was taken and we headed up to Sahagun. A town that is bigger than the others. It was time for lunch and time to rest. The previous night's lack of sleep was catching up on me and I was tired. We ate pasta and again we were about to set off when I heard shouts of "aqui, aqui" from along the street. There was only one person that could be and I looked back to see the ever-smiling face of Thomas the Swede. His favourite word of "aqui", which means everything in his own special way but "here" in Spanish, was echoing down the street. He had stayed at another town the previous night. His high spirits always make the group smile and soon group photos were being taken and stories exchanged.

My Brazilian masseuse had left her flip flops at the albergue and I had taken them in case of seeing her and she passed by and I quickly waved them at her and I was met with a smiling face, a hug and what I can only presume was thank you, you most handsome funny King type man in Portuguese. I took this opportunity to tell her (as best I could) that I had €10 and the name of the albergue where I would be staying and made the massage sign. She smiled and said "si, si!"

Out if the town we headed and I walked with Steph the Vet. A lovely woman with one of those London accents that's rather nice. We had a lovely chat about this and that and as we do we gave each other fun abuse. Well mine was fun however I often wonder if she is kidding. The kms quickly passed and in what seemed no time we had arrived at Calzada del Coto. As we walked through this sleepy farming village I was soon to witness another Camino miracle. Eduardo the unlucky, go get em, funny Italian that we had left back in the last albergue was sitting there washed and laughing. I said did you get a bus? he laughed and said, "no no no I gee 3 keeos eend now we I deeestoy eeet" which I believes translates to "I gave away 3 kg of kit and now I destroy the Camino in that I can go fast" I didn't care how he had got here I just always like to see the guy who makes me laugh. I hugged him and he shouted behind me that the showers were great.

The albergue was cold and the showers were freezing. I didn't have a shower as I saw the bluish looking bodies come out. My feet were sore and I was really tired feeling. The thought of a rest day in Leon started to cross my mind. Could I afford a hotel for a couple of nights? I have the time. I will chew on the thought. We headed to the local bar where a few old men played cards. We ordered food and I smiled as just before I had left the albergue the Brazilian woman arrived. Could I get massage two nights in a row?

"You don't always need a plan. Sometimes you just need to breathe, trust, let go, and see what happens." ~ Mandy Hale

back - The Ausies, Tiger, Alex, Elea, Tim, Steph, Becky. Front - Thomas, me and Eduardo

# Day 20

## A letter with courage
## Calzada del Coto to Reliegos

Three weeks have passed since I had bid farewell to my dad at the airport and as I awoke this morning to a very chilly room I felt refreshed and well slept. My lack of sleep the night before and my second massage of my Brazilian friend helped me sleep all the way to at least 7ish. We drank a coffee that was given by the hospitalero with some pieces of readymade toast and butter. There was a walk of 8.5 km till we could stop and find coffee.

It was a beautiful morning even though a frost was evident and I wished everyone a Buen Camino and a second later I heard "hey wait for me"! The Italian accent was unmistakable and of course it was my great friend Eduardo. We headed out of town and it was obvious it was all rich farmland and the farms sat next to the Camino with the occasional tractor passing by as it headed to a many acre field for its day work. I waved at all the tractors that passed and each driver would give a hearty wave back. I wondered if the farmers were as friendly during the summer when there are thousands of pilgrims walking along the dusty Camino/farmers roads. I like to think they are.

Eduardo and I had walked briefly together but not like this. We have laughed often and I he is such a likeable guy and his English is getting better and we started chatting. Within a few kms we were discussing life and parts of our lives had a similarity that allowed us both to be open and honest with each other. There was a definite understanding of the issues and some of the choices both of us had made in life and here we were, two guys from different parts of the world and even through broken but not bad English we could relate. It was great to talk and listen to Eduardo's story. As it's not my story to tell I can only think and be grateful that he shared it with me. Not too different from myself.

The day was warming up and our conversation was just about to also. After Eduardo had told me his story I said is that why you came on the Camino. He then proceeded to tell me that no it was not the reason. My ears were perking and listening to every word he said. He said in a soft voice that his mother had died on the 25th January. I looked at him and said, "you mean this January just passed" and he said yes. Eduardo had not mentioned this to anyone and I felt my eyes start to well up. Here was this great guy who had had nothing but challenges since he started still getting on with it and his mum had just passed. He looked at me and with a nervous laugh said this "my mum gave me a letter before she died and I didn't have the courage to open it until last week. After reading it, it has given me the courage to carry on and do this" a tear rolled down my cheek and I put out my hand and grabbed his and shook it in a I just know kind of way. Eduardo's story had touched me and his bravery that he continued to show was an inspiration for anyone. I didn't ask what was in his mother's letter of course but I knew it had had an impact on him.

It was time to walk with the jacket off for the first time this trip. The sun was hot enough to disperse the chill coming in from the snowy peaks that were just coming into view. A few days away I thought but I have to cross them.

Eduardo and I talked more and he told me about his dreams and of finishing university one wish his mum had asked for in the letter he told me how grateful he was to have his girlfriend and how after everything that they had been through she would make a long journey to meet him when he finishes at the airport and spend a night with him. He just smiled and said it was romantic. It was indeed and I was for a second envious of that. To have someone you love waiting for you like that. Another Camino for me maybe.

As we walked into the town of Calzadilla de los Hermanillos it was like every other town that we walk into and was quiet. We could not find a shop or open bar and we split up and walked through the maze of small streets. It reminded me of a town in the Midlands with its brick work and I did run into two old Spanish people and made the international sign for hungry by rubbing my belly and using my imaginary knife and fork.

They replied with the international sign of wrong directions with a smile and a laugh. I somehow found Eduardo and the Australians who had found the smallest shop on the planet with the smallest and happiest shopkeeper. He had fresh cakes and other treats and we sat outside his shop with the stools he provided and let the sun warm our tired bodies. As we sat the rest of the group started to appear and tell us of a restaurant that had no food but did have coffee. The owner had told them to tell everyone to bring their food. So, we did.

The restaurant was great and we were all in good spirits that was helped with the owner who was a character and most apologetic that he did not have anything in as he was just opening for the season. That's happened a few times now I thought. We have timed it well. Some had a beer or two and some of us lay in the sun after eating cakes and chorizo. A strange combination. A group picture and we were off on the 17km track to the next and final town. That's a long way for one stretch but at that point I had not thought about it. We all headed out of town and Steph and I walked and chatted and as usual she had me chuckling at her witty cheekiness. About 4 kms in we all started to go at our own pace and I took this time to finally get my Pavarotti ultimate collection on and I set a pace. The road was straight and there was not much to see other than the mountains with the snow that twinkled on top of them far away in the distance. It was great though. The music played in the background as my thoughts for the first time in a couple of days had a chance to dance and I was soon daydreaming. What would it feel like to walk into Santiago? How were some of my new friends getting on? It would be sad to see the Brits go home in Leon but it's been so amazing to meet them, will I ever find "the one" again. The usual thoughts for me and they were good.

It seemed like a long afternoon and my feet were sore for the last 5km. It was hard to see the town and the reason being the town of Reliegos was in a dip so you didn't see it until you were on it. It was a great sight as the priest and I entered. A bar was spotted and we headed straight for it. A beautiful sight after that walk in the sun and we were met by the incredibly brilliant owner who seems to love everything about life. We sat and ate and soon the rest of our group started to arrive. Everyone was talking about how the last stretch was quite hard and the music played. Thomas from Sweden danced on the street and we all laughed. Life was good and we all knew it. The Camino delivers a sense of joy after every day. It's the Camino gods saying well done I think.

Leaving this amazing watering hole, we headed to the albergue which was €5 for the night. The bunks are joined together and I laughed as I said to my neighbour, Steph, that it would be nice to sleep next to a doctor as I had already slept with a teacher, a priest and a Canadian woman with whom I never even spoke to. Not bad for two weeks on the road I joked. The evening meal was cooked by the one and only Eduardo who cooked up a storm and served us all carbonara that was delicious. Another great day on the Camino. A special one in its own way but I have to be honest they have all been special in their own way.

"love the life you live. live the life you love." ~ Bob Marley

*The long straight road to Santiago*

# Day 21

## A treat is what you sometimes need
## Reliegos to Leon

The dinner that was cooked was beautiful however I had not been feeling one hundred percent since the end of the day so I lay on my bed for half an hour. I could feel the sickness feeling building and I got up to speak with the peeps in the kitchen. It was not long before I was hanging over the toilet being violently sick. I washed my face in cool water and I immediately felt fine. As if I had not been sick at all. I was happy with that and thought about what I could have eaten that made me feel like that. Toast with butter and Coke for breakfast, Coke with chorizo and crisps and a coffee for lunch and Eduardo's delicious pasta with lots of Coke. I fear my Coke intake may be too high and made note not to drink too much today. I went to bed after painting and listening to Tim and Alexandro debate a whole variety of subjects. It was fun and it was fun to tease Steph when I got in the bunk with a "high honey I'm home!". Two bunk beds together are like a king size bed though and we had joked that there was a passport control where the beds met. The sleep came and it was the norm toss and turn and the am arrived.

There was no breakfast in the little town we were in so the Brits, as it's their holiday, wanted to walk the scenic route. I said I would join them and upon discussion it was decided that the scenic route was back out of the town the way we had entered and then on. There was another option that was more direct that seemed better however off we went. Climbing the hill out of town, away from our destination of Leon, we soon concluded that we had to head back down the way we came and go the direct route. As we walked down the hill a flock of sheep walked down staring at us. I couldn't help but think that they were laughing with each other saying look at these lost Pellegrino's. This is a first. I'm sure one shouted "Hey Ewe are Ewe lost!"

After passing the sheep that were, I'm positive, laughing at us I found myself walking back into the town we had left half an hour before but from a different angle. This was the second time in this adventure I had went in a circle I thought. We passed through the town that looked completely different and found the Camino. The next goal was as always coffee and food. Off we strode.

We passed through the tiny village Villarmoros and onto Puente Villarente which was 6 km away. I could smell the coffee a mile away and Tim and I chatted as we walked. The Brits have been a lovely group to have met and I couldn't help but think that I'll miss them when they leave. That's the Camino though.

The stop was good and I was hungry after being sick the night before so toast and jam was washed down with coffee and orange juice followed by tortilla and bread. It was delicious and I was ready to head on.

We left the eating place and walked through the "door of St James" the ruin wall that remains and is where every pilgrim who walked the French Way passed through. I stood there and touched the stones trying to get some sense of the thoughts, dreams, desperation and all other emotions that had passed through this very spot. There are a few places on the Camino that I have experienced this and I like to think and imagine. Right before the gate a great sculpture shows tired modern day pilgrims resting. It struck a chord and we all laughed at the expression and body language as we were exactly the same.

As we headed through the town I realised that my headphones that were supposed to be around my neck were not there. These were not just any headphones but the ones I had bought from the barman when I had lost the last pair. Earlier that morning when passing an albergue the three Dutch women we keep running into came and shouted on me. They had my earphones. It was the woman who's socks I had found that had found my earphones! The Camino gods had returned them for passing the sock test yet no more than an hour later they were gone again. I headed back to the cafe as the others went on. Alex,

Elea and the priest were coming out of the cafe as I approached and they laughed and asked what I'd lost this time. I have a reputation I thought. After searching the cafe still nothing and we headed off towards the gate to the city. Just before the gate I saw the earphones on the ground. They were back after being washed twice, tumble dried twice and lost twice. I was happy.

We headed out of town towards the next towns of Arcahueja and Valdelafuente and Alex and I were chatting and I was reconfirming a few things like Jesus was a prophet in this faith, God in another and a false prophet in another. I was trying to get my head round this vast subject and it was interesting. We passed through a small town and an old man had opened his garage to put his car away. Alex and I stared in disbelief as the old chap had glamour (non nude) calendars that were poster size covering his garage. I reckon they must have been from the 1980's. Alex and I had fallen behind as at one point I had went to check what time it was. We were about 12 km into the day and there was no watch on my wrist. I couldn't believe it and I quickly recalled when I'd last seen it. When I went to bed I took it off and when I left this morning there was nothing on my bed. Rucksack quickly emptied and upon opening my clothes bag my watch fell on the ground. I said to Alex that I think the Camino gods are just having a laugh now. This was reinforced as I then explained to Alex that my bed sheet was still in the albergue from the previous night to last as I'd forgotten that. This just fuelled the Iain forgets stuff joke and even more the "do you have" question then a list of items read off by everyone daily. I was happy to have my watch though and we headed into town and caught up with everyone at our second stop. Some chorizo and coffee with a side of chips that was washed down with magnum ice cream white chocolate magnificence and I was off for the next 12 km into the city of Leon.

Many of the little villages in this area have houses and walls made with mud and straw. These were interesting to see and gave me a sense of what it must have been like and still is for some to live in this area. Thomas the Swede and I walked together for a few kms and it was nice as not much was said. Just companions walking. What he did tell me though was that he was involved with running a band and showed me pictures of him in China last year and it reminded me of when I first met him and he raved about King Tuts Wah Wah Hut in Glasgow. Thomas is a cool guy with the heart of a young man.

We were soon leaving the countryside and starting to come into the outskirts of Leon. Steph, my bunk bed partner, and I walked and as normal she gave me witty banter and I was even wittier back. I'll miss Steph and her unique personality. She has a great heart although tried to pretend she doesn't. You can't kid a kidder I've often thought. We walked and talked and as always laughed and soon we were walking through the streets of Leon with the others in the group. It's nice to be in a big city and watch the hustle and bustle. We did an Abbey Road type picture and the conversation was all about a rest day. I had decided that after twenty-one days of walking I was staying two nights in Leon. We arrived at the albergue and there was a bar opposite. Non-alcoholic beer with cheese and bread. What could be better than this I thought.

As some headed for the albergue some of us had decided to treat ourselves. I went online and booked myself a room in a hotel next door to the albergue. The king bed with whirlpool bath was just what the Dr ordered. I was in heaven and I spent time treating my wee feet, that were starting to show hot spot, to a good soak and some relaxation. Bliss. I sent a message to the guys in the albergue if anyone wanted a bath. Not with me of course. With themselves. The Priest arrived and disappeared into the bathroom saying he had never had a whirlpool bath. Good deed for the day complete.

It was hard to drag myself off the top of my amazingly comfy bed to go meet everyone for dinner. I looked over at the priest, who was hanging out after his bath and sitting on the reclining seat catching up on whatever with the use of the Wi-Fi. I said, "I guess we had better head" and had a chuckle to myself as I knew I would have fun telling everyone that not only had the priest slept with me but had a bath in my room. Tiger the priest has a great sense of humour and laughs a lot and hard. He will no doubt be a great man in his life and inspire many.

We waited outside the hotel for the arrival of the Brits who were twenty minutes late and of course arrived with smiles and a "oh I thought it was 7.30". They do make me chuckle. We headed into the heart of Leon and its nightlife and restaurant district. It's beautiful with narrow streets and small bars that can fit twenty people at a crush. The cool night air felt exquisite on my feet as I walked around in my sandals letting my toes breath and relax.

I was hungry and as the group were deciding what they wanted to do I was being a little impatient and saw a kebab shop. Yes, I thought and I jumped in to ask for a small donnar. It was quickly served and as I met the others there were four pilgrims who we had met earlier on the Camino talking to them. They looked at my donnar and said with eyes wide open and an accent hardly recognisable due to immediate heavily saliva flow "where you get that" I pointed and in a flash, they were gone as their hungry feet marched them onwards to food heaven.

The group had decided that pizza was the dish for the day and we sat and enjoyed some amazing pizza followed by a chocolate desert of sort that tasted incredible. Heading back to my room I was ready to relax and relax I did.

*"Wake up, smile and tell yourself Today is my day!" ~ Unknown*

# Day 22

Rest day - we all need a rest now and then
Leon

Waking up a couple of times and going back to sleep was brilliant in my comfy bed and just after 8am I felt well and truly refreshed. Alex had sent a message at 6.30am to say that they had to be out of the albergue by 8am (which is normal) I pulled some clothes on and set out into the city to see if I could find them so that they could leave their bags in my room.

The nightlife district had a massive number of bottles and cups covering the ancient streets and a Spanish gent hosed the trash down the street under the morning sun. I had no idea where everyone would be however on walking into a main square I ran into, Becky who is one of the Brits, and we headed towards the cathedral for a look. As we entered the square I could see everyone and good morning hugs and words of joy to see each other were exchanged. The cathedral was closed at this early hour as was, what seemed to be, everything. I thought siesta was only in the afternoon. We all headed off to find breakfast and we did. Some tortilla with bread, coffee and orange juice. It was lovely and I headed back to my hotel. I wanted to use the bath one more time and relax while I could. The bath was incredible and I took the time to speak with pops and give my friend Junie a call to hear the banter. All was good at home and all was good here. With the bath robe on I lay back on the bed for a cheeky thirty-minute nap.

I awoke and drank the remainder of two bottles of water as it had been highlighted to me by my friend that I needed to drink more water. I couldn't argue with her so started the day the right way. I packed my rucksack and walked the ten doors along the hotel to ask Thomas from Sweden if I could leave my things there till later and of course he said yes. A real nice guy.

I met with the theologian, his wife and the priest and we headed into the narrow streets of Leon on our way to the Cathedral. The streets and buildings I love as they are so close and tight and all with café's and bars. When we reached the cathedral, it was €5 to go in and no discount for pilgrims so I decided I didn't need to see the inside. Neither of us went in and we got some history from Alex anyway so that was good and I loved the outside. From here we started walking and soon Steph from the Brits stopped us. Small world indeed. The Brits were having a couple of wines and I went and said hi before the group set off. Our goal was to buy a poncho.

We stopped at a chocolate shop and the others had fancy chocolate drinks however Eduardo who like a magician had just shown up -and I drank coffee as the others went for the sugar high. Away we set again towards the poncho shop and

I couldn't help but love the day of rest we were all having. My body was thanking me as was my brain and I was enjoying looking at the buildings and everyday life of this beautiful city. I remembered the shepherd I had seen with his flock just outside the city the day before. His dog and him letting his sheep and goats graze on a piece of land as the trucks and city stole the rich land around them. It was a great sight and I wondered if the shepherd ever wandered into the city and what his thoughts were. We walked on passed Elvis who was in his plastic cut out glory and some fountains that were spectacular. One of the fountains saw a statue of a man holding a dagger. He was Alonso Pérez de Guzmán known as Guzmán el Bueno ("Guzmán the Good") and basically back in the day he had promised the King to hold the fort. When it was attacked, the enemy found and brought his son to the fort to say surrender or we'll kill your son. This guy takes out his dagger and throws it to the enemy and says well use this to kill him. While an honourable thing to do, I was told I couldn't help but think it was a bit stupid. A sad story really.

On arrival at the sporting goods shop they showed me an amazing poncho that was €65. I declined and went for the €15 one that was similar to the one I had lost. It will do the job over the next two weeks I thought.

On our way back, we ran into the Brits. The others went to the albergue to sleep. I picked up my things as I now had a new hotel room. The Brits had a spare bed in their fancy place and I had won the golden ticket to have a second night in a comfy bed. Could I fit in an extra and third bath? My rest day had been a busy one in the sense of seeing the city and I was looking forward to a rest. First, I sat with the Brits and had a nice chat as always and then I was taken to my room for the evening. It was a lovely place and I lay on the bed looking for a quick snooze and in what was no time I was awakened to say it was time to go and meet everyone. I was in a comfy zone and I didn't want to move but the twenty-five minutes or so was good and I headed out with the Brits, who are on their last night, to meet up with the group. Tonight was going to be a special night in Leon and I could feel something in the air. It is soon to be Easter and the parades were about to start.

We reached the bar and the rounds of drinks were flowing and the chat was all about what next, how long it will take and the last night of the Brits. It will be sad to see them go. The time was coming on 8pm and the bar that was busy started to empty and as I looked out I saw the square was full. The parade "Friday of Sorrows" was starting and I headed out. There was a really eerie feeling as the church bells from the churches around began their chorus. They literally sang of sorrow and echoed off the buildings. The slow beat of the drums soon became apparent and the horns from the brass instruments played a slow sombre tune. The Friday of Sorrows gives the idea that the Virgin also suffers for the Holy Week and it is a huge deal here by the looks of it. As the procession slowly passed, a huge statue of the Virgin carrying Christ that was supported by men passed by. Women were dressed in traditional Spanish clothes that they wear when going to church. As the Virgin passed the whole procession swayed back and forth and I'd be lying if I didn't say it was powerful stuff. I'd never seen anything like this and I'll never forget it.

As I walked back to the hotel it was raining and the bars of Leon were spilling onto the street. I liked this city and the Brits and I stopped at a bar and then a chocolate place before heading back to the comfiness of the hotel. I had enjoyed my rest day with everyone and now I was tired and hungry and as the clock struck 11pm I thought of the others who were in the albergue and most likely asleep. I was with the Brits however and enjoying the banter and company. I liked them and they had been a big part of the Camino journey. Becky the human jukebox had given me the use of a bath right after I met them, Tim and his quite amazing banter and calming and interesting chat was a daily delight and Steph the girl who consistently gave me a hard time in the funniest of ways had also given up a spare bed for me on my rest day so I could relax. She had become a good friend in the short time we knew each other. She is also the cheekiest person I know which always made me laugh as it was done with such finesse. A special rest day in Leon in many different ways. A city I hope I'll visit again one day. Tomorrow though the Camino continues.

"Sometimes we become so focused on the finish line, that we fail to find joy in the journey." ~ Dieter F. Uchtdorf

*Leon Cathedral*

# Day 23
## Friends depart and the Camino dreams on
## Leon to Villar de Mazarife

I awoke inside the comfy covers of my four-star gifted hotel bed. I had slept well and it was nearly 8am. The others were meeting me at the coffee shop by 8.30am. The Camino was again back in my thoughts and I packed my bags while wondering why I had not taken advantage of the bath the previous night as it may be some time before I see another one. Tiredness had won that battle. As I had run out of shampoo I thought it only correct to ask Steph if she required the hotel supplied goodies and as she didn't I thought it only correct as a pilgrim to carry them on towards Santiago to keep me clean. I bid farewell to Steph and headed to meet the others at the coffee shop. Shared experiences is what Steph always used to say. I smiled.

I met everyone, and we were all were smiles except my great Swedish friend Thomas. I could see something was on his mind and as I sat with my coffee, orange juice and pastry he said to me he needed to go faster and that he wanted to tell the group that he had to go on a different route than we were going that day. The Camino had two choices today and we took the longer scenic route. Thomas told the group that he had to split and as with the Camino we would also soon have to say Buen Camino to our great friend. It's the way of the Camino. You meet people and build a relationship and then they are gone. The Camino however has a crazy way of bringing people back together again. You say goodbye then a few days later you bump into them randomly in a town. It's a tough lesson to learn when you say farewell to people however the Camino will deliver a soothing and comforting arm around your shoulder by introducing new people and new sights as soon as you're on the way again. I wondered if people fell in love on the Camino or if they fell in love with the Camino. I feel I may be the latter although my romantic side is not averse to the first thought.

We all set off through the city of Leon passing the outstanding 13th Century cathedral and other amazing buildings. The old monastery that is now a parador (a hotel) and statues that showed pilgrims resting. Of the large cities I had passed through, Pamplona, Burgos and Leon, I said to Thomas that I would like to visit this city again. It was for me the prettiest so far. I had to remember though that my judgement may have been swayed by two nights of nice beds. The walk out of the town had us singing a few songs and I had changed the words to "it's a long way to Tipperary" to

> "It's a long way to Santiago
> It's a long way to go
> It's a long way to Santiago
> With my new friends I go
> Goodbye Pamplona
> Farewell Leon too
> It's a long long way to Santiago
> And my heart is true"

Eduardo especially liked this and I spent some time going slowly with him as he mastered it in the correct English. He had done this the night before with a toast I had said that he liked. He couldn't get it at the time but was quite clear when he repeated it to me as we walked. The boy has a talent I thought as he said in his Italian accent. "Listen"[to the toast] "Here's to you and here's to me, best of friends we'll always be, If by chance we disagree, Then f*%k you and here's to me" He laughed a lot as he said it. One of the songs I had sang for fun a few days back was one that we sang as kids on the school trips we took and possibly may only be funny in Scotland and to people under the age of 16 however I sang it and the theologian and the priest liked it and laughed. Now the strange thing is the priest now sings it daily and laughs his head off. I sometimes look and think that the priest will have so many stories when he gets back to Korea. The song was.

*"I want my hol, I want my hol, I want my holidays*
*To see the count, to see the count, to see the country*
*Fo Q, Fo Q for Curiosity*
*I want my hol, I want my hol, I want my holiday"*

Sung like a Scottish school kid it doesn't quite sound the way it is written but it's hilarious as the priest sings it and he knows what it's saying – I think.

We passed out of Leon and into the outskirts of the city which like any city changes from magnificent splendour into the living areas where the thousands of people have their home and make it the city it is. We reached the town of Valverde de la Virgen which is where the split with Thomas would be and we ate French toast and had a coffee. With hugs and wishes of the best kind we said farewell to Thomas. I wasn't too sad as I knew I'd meet him again. Another great human walking the Camino.

We were now back to a small group of four, the theologian, his wife Elea, the priest and myself. Of course, there was also Eduardo the Italian and he would be somewhere as he left with us, passed us smiling saying he "had the energy" and went into the mist with a spring in his step. He would be seen again that's for sure. The rain had started and I was happy that I had walked the 2km the day before to purchase my poncho. It was warm though so I laughed to myself at wearing all the keep myself dry gear when the truth was I was soaking wet from the inside out. I made a note to wash my clothes when I reached my destination. We left and the Camino split into the scenic route and the road route. It was a bit confusing but we were soon on the scenic route.

There was hardly any talk and the four of us split and went at our own pace. I didn't want to listen to music and was happy to walk the remaining 12 km with my thoughts. I remember thinking holy shit if I could capture my thoughts for the last five minutes I could write a lot of books. I thought of many things. I was thinking about rules and how people set rules and we follow them for many different reasons and that in another culture they are completely different. An obvious thought however my thoughts went deeper and deeper into the subject. I thought of a book I'd like to write and the plot. I have written a lot of it in my head and even I can't wait for what happens next. The Camino has inspired my thriller mixed with love of course. And of course, I thought of love as I always do and drank water as I had been told to by a friend. The scenery was a mixture of crops starting to slowly come through the reddish soil and flat fields of grass. We entered the village of Chozas de Abajo hoping that the bar was open however like every sleepy Spanish village there was no one around. Resting I took the opportunity to use nature's bathroom and was stunned to see the biggest bird nest I've ever seen. These huge birds were perched on it and as I proceeded with my nature calls routine it suddenly dawned on me and I hoped these big birds did not mistake something I was holding for a worm and make a beeline for it. Again, we headed off on our own towards the town were staying in. My feet and especially my heels/Achilles were aching, and I thanked myself for building in extra days that meant I could rest when I needed to. I would need to go easy as I have some hard, long uphill days ahead I thought. Just then the town came into view. I was happy and my phone beeped with a message from Eduardo "albergue Jesus good, Wi-Fi good, warm and supermarket x2." Where we were staying was sorted and I checked in. The room was for four and it was warm. The shower was good and I washed my clothes in it. Eduardo was cooking again and I relaxed with a non-alcohol beer on my own in the bar. Today I had said goodbye to some special people and I was grateful I had met them but I was also happy to be on the Camino again and walking. I had to be in Santiago at some point and it was pulling me closer with its magnetic grip on my soul. My heart longed for it and I was happy. My Camino Dream was indeed alive.

> *"You can't start the next chapter of your life if you keep re-reading the last one."* ~ Michael McMillan

# Day 24
## Much kindness shown
## Villar de Mazarife to Astorga

The night had been good with Eduardo cooking his homemade pasta with four cheeses. The five of us sat and ate till our bellies were full. After dinner I was feeling tired so had another shower as they were good and lay on my bed for a while contemplating how far to go next. After various options, I reverted back to the "I'll go until my feet say that's it for the day" mode. After this revelation, that I have on a daily basis, I headed back to the gang who were deep in thought as they played their strategy out in a game of dominoes. Excited, but not showing it, they asked if I knew how to play. I, of course, said I didn't. They were not to know I captained the mighty funky Royal Bar B team to win the league back in the day. I was a shark and Alex, my partner in crime, could see it in my eyes and said he was a beginner also with a wink. We were ready to teach the Korean and Italian a lesson or two as we started playing. I picked up my first hand and could not see the dominoes for spots. We played and the youngsters were winning game after game and letting it be known with high fives and the Italian saying, "We destroy you." I watched and learned then with a knowing smile to Alex we set about playing for real. It was not long until the youngster's high fives had stopped and the Italian was now saying "I can't believe this" and "this is not possible aaahhhh". Sometime later we were shaking hands and as victors, Alex and I, celebrated with finesse. We all retired to our room and chatted for a bit. I was tired and soon the dreams would come but not before I had written a wee poem about love.

### AMOUR

*A simple word can make my day*
*A photo but a week*
*A call to me would make my year*
*You are the one I seek*

*Afar you are but what's a mile*
*Afar the miles are more*
*Afar the oceans I must swim*
*So much I miss it's sore*

*But you are there and I must dream*
*But what if it could change*
*But these are dreams that can be seen*
*This feeling is not strange*

*You are the one I seek*
*So much I miss it's sore*
*This feeling is not strange*

*The word is just amour.*

The morning saw me take a shower. A do not do as your feet get wet and soft they say. I had lots of time to dry them though and I looked at the guide as we were heading to Santibanez de Valdeiglesia which was about 21km away. It was raining however I had all my waterproofs on and I set off alone with some good music playing in my ears. The first 6km was a straight road then there was a slight bend and then it was straight again for the next 4km. I was enjoying some me time and I passed a group of Spanish women who had stayed at the albergue. I made good time and my feet were good as I entered the village of Villavante looking forward to a coffee or juice. There was nothing open so I strode on towards the town of Hospital de Orbigo.

The rain had stopped as I entered the village of Puente de Orbigo which sits on the far side of Hospital de Orbigo. The main thing that you see if a beautiful bridge. It dates from the 13th century and is one of the longest and best preserved medieval bridges in Spain. There is a great story to be told here. As you pass over the bridge you pass over the passage of honour or Palo Thorson. So called because in 1434 a famous jousting tournament took place here. A noble knight from Leon, Don Suero de Quiñones, scorned by a beautiful lady threw down the gauntlet to any knight who dared pass as he defended the bridge and his honour. Knights from all over came to joust and he defended the bridge for a month until he had collected the three hundred lances that had been broken. He then rode to Santiago to offer thanks for his freedom from the bonds of love and for his honour, now restored. I liked the story and tried to imagine the craziness of these knights jousting and what the scenes must have been like.

I stopped off for a coffee and pastry as I had walked a fair bit yet it was still early and I was only 5 km away from my destination. It was delicious and I decided that if my feet were OK I'd walk on to Astorga which was another 17 km away. I knew the others in the group did not want to go that far but I thought to myself that this is "my way" and if I wanted to push on then they would understand. I also have learned that you always meet up with people again so off I set.

Minutes after leaving the restaurant I heard a familiar Italian voice. The bold Eduardo was there and I explained to him I was going to Astorga and he said he was going too and off we went chatting about the Moto GP. Eduardo is a massive Moto GP fan and there is only one Italian rider he talks about, Valentino Rossi. His hero and he talked in depth about how he hated the Spanish riders and various things about racing. He asked a few people along the way if it was on TV. We passed through the village of Villares de Orbigo and onto where we were meant to stay, Santibanez de Valdeiglesia. There were a lot of day trippers walking and I liked seeing the people walk The Way. We stopped at the albergue we were going to stay at and drank a sugar free Coke, ate an apple and filled out water bottles. It was only 1pm so the decision to keep going was the right one as my feet were good and the weather was now good.

As we headed out of town there were a few young cows in a pen and I spoke Spanish Coo to them. One was licking my hands and liking it due to the salt from my sweat and it was great as Eduardo had never let a cow lick him. He was amazed by the roughness of the tongue and we laughed hard as the sun began to get hotter and we moved on. The day was getting better by the minute as usual.

We headed on and the path was insanely muddy and the mud stuck to our boots like it was a special type of chewing gum. The plus side was it was soft underfoot so my feet were happy and the scenery was pretty with more hills now. That wonder of what's over the next crest is always good. After making my mark with stones on the way with the letters "KOS" we came over the brow of a hill and came upon a place where they had a little cart with fresh fruit and juice sitting there. We stopped and were greeted by a young man originally from Barcelona who said, "no charge please eat and take what you want." The act of kindness I loved and the place where he, a girl called Suzie and an older guy lived was all about love and being good to people. All that they asked for was that you walked with your heart. I took my rucksack off and sat down with fresh strawberries and a banana. I don't normally eat strawberries as I am not that into them, but they tasted beautiful. I know I'll eat them often now and I'll always think of this place that was just perfect.

We left and walked with a young Irish girl called Helen for a bit. It was her second day and she was pleasant as we passed by a cross that overlooked the city and some more statues. We chatted about reasons we were here and some of the stories of what The Way had been like so to help Helen a little.

Stopping for a snack at a bar in the town of San Justo de la Vega we ate what I can only describe as the best Tortilla I've had on the Camino. It was so tasty and I savoured every part. The barman was friendly and he introduced us to Conchi a beautiful Spanish woman who was so friendly and chatted to us about her time visiting Glasgow and Edinburgh. She talked about when she had done the Camino and how she will again one day. The barman gave us the local meat to try and it was just an amazing stop. Again, it is the people who make it.

We set of for the last few kms to town and received a text from the Priest. They had decided to walk on also which surprised me so I knew I'd see them soon. The town of Astorga came close and Eduardo and I walked through the corn as it seems to be a well grown crop in these parts and soon we saw the theologian and his wife Elea along with the priest behind us and they caught up to reach the albergue for the night.

It was the longest walk so far (31km) and I loved it. My feet were good and the day seems free. I checked into a room and it turned out I was sharing with a father and son from Belfast who are walking and cycling due to time. They have raised over £3000 and it's for fresh water in Africa. The name that Mike had come up with for fundraising I loved. It came after he learned that a person could walk for five miles for a bucket of water and as the Camino is five hundred miles they called their fundraiser "100 buckets of water." Michael, the son even washed my gear which was very kind. It was time to go see what the city offered for food. I passed a bar where Eduardo was glued to the to screen watching the Moto GP and met up with the others and the Australians who had reached here a day earlier. I passed a parade that was happening and again it was great to watch the culture of this great country unfold in front of me. 31km of new and amazing things.

*"Whenever you find yourself doubting how far you can go, just remember how far you have come. Remember everything you have faced, all the battles you have won, and all the fears you have overcome." ~ Unknown*

# Day 25

## Please no blisters
## Astorga to Rabanal del Camino

I awoke after a fairly decent night's sleep which had started with a couple of episodes of Still Game while lying in bed. I was chuckling away as my roommates snored away. I spoke with the others and we were meeting the Australians for the start so I headed outside. There I ran into my new French friend Celia. Celia is a girl we had met at the previous albergue and she was really quite funny. The night before we had been in the kitchen area and as I was doing my daily painting she asked to look through my previous ones and at the one with the arrow and KOS she exclaimed "ah, you are KOS". In the original photo, it was an arrow of stones with her name in stones and I added KOS. She had wondered who that was and there we were in a random kitchen laughing over our names being in stones together and never meeting. The Camino can help you laugh at the smallest of things on a daily basis. We took a selfie and then moved on to meet the rest of the group and we took a group selfie. Shortly after we met the Australians who were rested after their extra night in town and we took another selfie but with the Americans also. We moved through the main square where I saw some others I knew and we got a mega selfie and everyone was laughing. In the space of a 100m I was standing laughing with a Mexican, German, Italian, South Korean, two Australians, two Americans, two South Africans, a French and, of course, Scotland representation. People from all over the world and all heading to the same place. I love this coming together of people. Leaving Astorga we passed its impressive cathedral and the quite beautiful Palacio Episcopal which is Gaudi designed. We all headed off and some of us stopped for our morning coffee and pastry before leaving to head to our destination of Rabanel which was only 20 km away.

I headed of on my own and the music was on and my energy was high. The map had shown a rise of around 1000ft but it didn't look steep. I thought of the woman who proudly held the Astorga football scarf at the place we ate and wondered if I should set up the Scottish Astorga supporters club. Before I knew it, I had visions of Scottish Astorga supporters heading over to Spain for a fun long weekend. It was a pleasant walk out of the town until I started feeling a burning sensation on my right foot. I walked a little hoping it was just the way I had put my socks on but remembered reading that if you felt a hot spot then stop and deal with it. So I did. I stopped and whipped my boot and sock off and gave my hot spot a bit of a massage and put something on it when the Australians appeared. They had tape and Iain was down applying it to my feet in no time. I couldn't help but think that I have been incredibly blessed so far as things just seem to work out. I put it down to my sacrifices to the Camino gods and remembered that I had given them a pair of gloves somewhere along the Camino yesterday. Some laugh at me but I know that you have to give the gods an offering of something now and then. My feet taped and boots tight I thanked the Aussies and headed off. I phoned pops and we chatted and caught up as I passed through Murias de Rechivaldo and on a straight steady climb towards the next village which was about 6k away. I was walking at a decent pace and enjoying the energy as I rose higher and the views of the mountains that are tomorrow came into sight. There was one with snow on it and some with none and I thought I wonder where the pass will be. I'll find that out tomorrow.

I enjoyed this alone walking time and my thoughts were of some friends back home and around the world who have major stuff going on. I hoped and know that things will work out for them and wished I could magic them all to the Camino for a short period of their life. It would help them I thought. I know it's helped me in ways that I will try and explain one day. Pops had told me that someone from home wants to pick my brain about the Camino as they would like to do it and I thought about this and liked the idea. I thought of how I could tell people about my journey and experience but in a way that if they do it, it will be their own Camino with a few hints and tips I've picked up along the way. If I could spark just a tiny bit of the Camino flame in people I know that I'd enjoy watching their experience.

I was moving fast and I soon reached the village of Santa Catalina de Somoza. It was still early and I had covered 9.5 km so I decided not to stop for a coffee as I had had one less than two hours previous. It was a pretty village though and there were about three places to eat just as you entered. There were a lot of new faces also walking and many with day packs. I wondered if they were just doing a day or getting their packs moved ahead. Either way I pressed on and there was a village about 4km ahead that I'd stop at.

Moving on, the road was again a straight road across the plateau at the top of the hill. My pace was still quite fast and I was enjoying it when in no time the small village of El Ganso came into view and there was a bar called the Cowboy bar that I had decided I'd stop at. The village was small with some ruined houses but right in the heart was the cowboy bar. There was a group of women just arriving and I entered and ordered tortilla and coffee. I set it down and used the facilities to come back to find three of the women sitting where my coffee was so I said hello and it turned out they were Irish. Well we were soon all chatting and a few laughs were exchanged. There are eight ladies and one man in their group and I joked about the poor man having to do it with eight women. They were lovely ladies and they come every year and do a week of walking. So eventually they will get to Santiago. I loved that some have come for a few years and each time adding another bunch of kms to their pilgrimage. They said next year they hope to reach Santiago.

After some non-alcoholic beer for the nutrients I only had 4km to my stop point and it was still not noon. I thought I could go on but my feet would be requiring rest so off I went and passed some pilgrims along the way. I passed a guy who had what was like an old shopping bag on wheels I used to see as a kid. I just thought well it's his way and passed on by. About 2k from the town I met up with Phil who was one of the Irish ladies and we were both setting a good pace and off we went till we reached the town of Rabanal del Camino. We were heading to the same albergue and we were soon walking into the place to an old lady (mum I'm told) welcoming us and all smiles. Daughter of said mum completed our paperwork and payment and was amazingly friendly. It was only around 1pm but a rest was required. As first in the albergue I felt it necessary to test the showers and they were exquisite. I showered and changed. Soon others started to arrive. First the Irish contingent and later my Camino friends. Iain the Aussie picked the bunk that joins me so tonight I add sleeping with an Australian to my growing list of Camino sleeping buddies. My French friend arrived and gifted me her tea as tomorrow is her last day. A lovely gesture and I spent the next hour or so drinking tea next to a log fire writing and chatting to others who passed. It was nice to relax and give the feet a rest.

Hunger was chapping on the door of my belly so I headed off to the local bar where I ate a steak and cheese sandwich with coffee and then a packet of Doritos and then egg, sausage and

French fries were ordered with a Coke Zero. I ate every bit and my hunger was gone. Sleep beckoned and I knew that there was something special happening in the evening that I didn't want to miss. I would wait and see how I felt. I headed back to the albergue through this, as usual, beautiful Spanish village.

The evening had produced yet another first for me as most of the albergue were going to the church. The reason being is the Benedictine Monks do some chanting as a blessing for pilgrims. I was really tired however headed over to this twelfth century church that was, I believe, built by the Templars. As I entered I was again blown away by the inside. This was no grand church and it was well in need of repair however the character of it was beautiful. The monks did their chanting and it was good to experience something quite spiritual. We headed back to the albergue and we all sat and drank tea and told stories around the fire. It was great. Celia the French girl continued to surprise me with her incredible sense of humour, Eduardo can take the simplest of stories and have everyone in hysterics. The two American girls were talking of destinations and we just had a good time.

> "Strength does not come from winning. Your struggles develop your strengths. When you go through hardships and decide not to surrender, that is strength."~ Mahatma Gandhi

# Day 26

## On top of the world
## Rabanal del Camino to Molinaseca

Awaking every hour, or more like twenty minutes, seems to be the norm for me till I get to exhaustion and I sleep for an hour or two straight. Usually it is due to my legs being twitchy and the odd pain in my feet. I was awake at 6.30am and decided to just get up and go for it when the sun rose. I think I woke a few people up as my stealth tactics in the dark are not the best. My Camino shell clattered against a metal radiator that would have woken a hibernating bear and then I was told that my torch on my phone was the brightest thing ever and these two things sent me into a fit of nervous hysterics. I'm sure the laughing woke up some people. I spoke with Celia the French journalist and Natalie the American as they performed medical treatment on Natalie's feet. It was 7.30am and I was off. Nothing had prepared me for today so when I went outside and the warm orange red sun peeked up over the horizon I looked and stared. I was in a complete moment.

I headed onwards and out through the small village and wondered what the monks would be doing. My goal though was the Cruz de Ferro. This is a tall iron cross that sits on top of the mountain and a place where you take a stone you have carried as an offering of love. The stone had been with me for a long time and today it was its day.

Onwards I headed till I reached the ghost town Foncebadon. It had been abandoned however with the increase over the years of pilgrims there are now a few very nice albergues mixed in with the ruins of yesteryear. I needed to eat and also needed to use the restroom urgently. This was the first time on The Way I had had a sore stomach and I was glad it happened in a town. I wiped my...... brow of sweat and sat down for a coffee happy that disaster had been prevented. I heard a message from my friend Junie and was laughing at her silliness so gave her a call as I drank my coffee and the ate the loveliest toast and marmalade.

Leaving the village, I continued to climb towards my goal and another friend messaged me. This was strange timing as I was on my way to the iron cross to say a few words about this very person along with a few others. St James was again delivering a day and it wasn't even 10am. I was now going through patches of snow and I could feel my heart pounding with the exercise plus the anticipation of doing my little ritual. Pilgrims have stopped there and said their bit for a long time.

I approached the cross and was surprised it was on the side of the road. There was no one about other than the taxi I had seen pass earlier. Two people stood entwined and obviously having a very personal moment. I recognised them as the South Africans I had met the night before. With a lump in my throat I stayed well back ensuring that they had whatever time they needed. They left in the cab and there I was. Standing at the Cruz de Ferro on my own under blue skies and I went into my rucksack and pulled out my rock. I had carried this everywhere for months, the stone was for a person. A person that was but a dream but yet a friend, it was for the people I had hurt and mistakes I'd made, it was for my mum and dad, my son and sister and for the few people I had let close to me through romance. I had thought often about what I'd say and I also knew I wanted to say a few things to all of them. A please forgive me and I hope I can make you all proud sort of moment.

I walked up the pile of stones and my forehead touched the pole. The tears, oh they flowed, and I literally hugged that standing dream and memory catcher. I thanked my friends who had been there throughout some tough times, I thanked my family and then I buried my stone with the love that I have for that special person also. I said some words and had a feeling of complete joy. St James had delivered yet again a magical moment and I got to do it all alone at this amazing place. I couldn't have dreamed it better.

With a skip in my step I headed towards the direction of the highest point of the Camino. As I strode along the road I was literally on cloud nine when out of the blue my stomach gurgled. I laughed nervously and continued to walk. It happened again but this time more severe. Great! I panicked! It's happening! I have a sore stomach and I'm at 5000ft. I quickly pulled my guide out to see how far the next town was. 6 km! There was no way I was making that. Sweating and going into contingency plan

4.2 in the "I really didn't think this would happen to me" book I noticed a miracle on my guide. There was an albergue at the top of the mountain and was not too far away. I could make it.

Relieved, I walked into the shack that was playing monk chants and had crosses all over it. Coffee was on offer for a donation amongst the trinkets. I thought I'd better buy a coffee before I asked to use the toilet. My stomach was now screaming at me. "Servicios" I said through gritted teeth and with a smile and an aqui aqui(meaning here here) he motioned to the outside. I was giving him the I don't know what you're pointing at when I saw it. The sign that said "Letrina" and he was pointing at the other side of the road. The sign was beautifully done I thought and I headed across the road doing my best impression of a penguin and I saw it. "The Letrina." It was a wooden hut on stilts that sat precariously on the side of the mountain road. I entered to find the out of place modern toilet roll holder empty. Not strange as I was on top of a mountain. I remembered I had something in my rucksack which was in the old wooden shack. Back across the road I hobbled and frantically found hankies I had brought.

Back again to the letrina and the full picture of my situation was unfolding. I looked in disbelief as a wooden lid covered whatever was below. My eyes were wide and I shook as I lifted the wooden lid. I was now playing the lead role in that scene from Slumdog Millionaire. It was an experience I'll never forget nor will I ever forget the sight (rhymes with...) I saw when I removed that wooden lid to expose the hole that opened onto the mountain floor. There had been many pilgrims use this facility before me. However, I laughed as I left. I thought St James you did that to give me an experience and that it did. My stomach was fine all day after that.

Soon I reached the highest point of the Camino. You have to walk away from the path a few hundred meters but the view was breathtaking. I stood there with my water. Just me and a view of the world all around me. It was perfect. It was a steep descent now and the next village of Acebo came into view. I could see flags and signs promoting new albergues. As I entered the village there was an outside seating area and it was warm so I ordered a hamburger sandwich with a coke and before I could say yum yum a local dog had joined me for lunch. The Irish women who are travelling came by and said hi as they headed inside to have a bite themselves.

As I left the village I couldn't help but think that it was quite beautiful. My music was on and I headed for the next village. I was thinking to myself that I've thought about loads of people while walking. Some fleeting thoughts and others great memories or just thoughts. Whenever I did this I'd think of more people. The village of Riego de Ambros came into view.

I wasn't expecting much as the entrance was a rundown looking place. I was completely wrong and this beautiful village showed of its cultural splendour amazingly well. It was like a movie set but real.

Following the signs, I was now going down steep rocky paths and I passed a young German couple I had met a few days earlier. They were nice and it made me smile that they were on this adventure together. My romantic heart kicked in and I thought you'd need to be really in love to do this with someone. Or maybe not. What do I know about love I chuckled.

The town of Molinaseca came into view and that was my destination. It had been a 25k day but worth every second. I strode into the town singing and I couldn't believe that every village was getting prettier. I navigated my way through the narrow main street towards my albergue and I was soon sitting in the sun drinking my non-alcoholic beer.

I checked in and lay down for a while. I messaged the others to say where I was staying but had heard nothing. Maybe they had stayed at the town before. The time passed and about two hours later after a great shower I saw the priest and the Italian walk up the street. They stayed at another albergue with the theologian and his wife. We chatted and they headed off and one of the American girls and I went to eat something. The night was cold and the sky beautiful as I headed back to the albergue. What an amazing day. Life was good.

"Life is amazing.
And then it's awful.
And then it's amazing again.
And in between the amazing and awful it's ordinary and mundane and routine.
Breathe in the amazing,
hold on through the awful,
and relax and exhale during the ordinary.
That's just living heart-breaking,
soul-healing,
amazing,
awful,
ordinary life.
And it's breathtakingly beautiful." ~ L.R. Knost

*Cruz de Ferro*

# Day 27

## Sick day has arrived
## Molinaseca to Ponferrada

I have become sick. Last night while at dinner I felt unwell again and by the time I returned to the albergue all bets were off. I suddenly had zero energy and I was shaking uncontrollably with the chills. I didn't have the energy to get out of bed unless I had to make it to the bathroom. It was a struggle. I was in my warm sleeping bag and fully clothed as if going for a day's walking and still shivering. On one of my trips to the bathroom I tried to negotiate the stairs with the lights out and whacked my big toe. This gave me a scare as I thought if this is sore in the morning then there will be no walking. I tried to sleep but it was a terrible night with little or no sleep. I was freezing then roasting hot repeatedly through the night.

I heard everyone getting up in the morning and I still had no energy so it took me a long time just to pack my rucksack. I thought to myself try and get to the next city and get a hotel. Thoughts of get a bus or a taxi, send your pack on and just book in somewhere in the town here came to mind often.

I didn't know what was wrong and the others were staying at a different albergue. The Australians passed where I was and I told them and they both immediately thought food poisoning. They headed off and the Irish girl Helen I had met a few days earlier gave me some medicine to replace my minerals etc.

Leaving last, I headed to the other albergue where the others were and told them that I was going to get a hotel and what had been going on. They are a great lot and we headed off to walk the 9km into the city. It was tough to say the least and I dreamed about just feeling better. The morning selfie was not a pleasant one and the tiredness oozed from my eyes.

The pace was slow and we reached the town where we met Chelsea who had stayed with us a couple of nights ago. She had gone on and was waiting for her friend who had been at the airport in Brussels when there was an attack. She was happy to see us and we went to a cafe.

I was looking at an amazing castle a Templar one but there was no excitement for me. My mind was exhausted as was my body. Had I bitten off too much I thought then I had a word with myself and thought no. It's a simple fact of food poisoning. Note to self, do not buy a hamburger again. When I was drinking lots of Coke this didn't happen I laughed to myself.

As we were sitting in the cafe the theologian and his wife, the Priest and the crazy Italian all decided they were staying also. How could I be so lucky to meet such great people. I was secretly quite overwhelmed by their simple act of kindness.

Elea wanted to taste Crepes and I liked the idea so we walked to the crepe place which was about 1.5km away and through a market. I was really struggling now but through my heavy eyes it was nice to see the market and the traders doing what our ones do by shouting their deals while women clustered around fresh produce prodding and poking it in full discussion of what is the best quality for the price they paid. We arrived at the crepe place and I ordered something sweet but was unable to eat it due to it tasting not so good. The others liked theirs however my hotel was now booked so I bid them farewell and headed the distance back to the hotel where I checked in and literally hit the pillow sleeping.

I woke about three and a half hours later and still felt bad. I drank a sachet I had bought from the pharmacy that replaced minerals and replied to the messages I had from my friends asking if I needed anything. A short while later Alexandro and Elea arrived with the bananas and water I had asked for. I'm in bed feeling sorry for myself and hoping I'll be ok tomorrow so I can get on the road. I will however not walk if I'm not feeling good. I was thinking that you should be able to rent a nurse and then laughed and thought you probably could but not in the caring type way. I am totally useless at being sick. I personify what man flu is in the mind of most people. Here is to sleep and a better day tomorrow.

"When 'I' replaced with 'We', even the illness becomes wellness." ~ Malcolm X

# Day 28

## What a difference a day makes
## Ponferrada to Villafranca del Bierzo

The night was not something I had been looking forward to however with my own room, one and a half litres of pure water, stomach tablets and four bananas I knew I was just where I needed to be and I would not leave this small but beautiful sanctuary for the next nineteen hours. I had slept and then dosed and drank the minerals then ate a little and consumed water. This along with great Wi-Fi which let me watch a few episodes of Still Game that kept me smiling through my less frequent chills. It was nice to see the lovely messages people had sent me and when you're away from home they just seem that little bit more special when you are not feeling the best. I switched to documentaries and caught up on the news on BBC World 24. Just tragic what has happened in Brussels.

My night went well with one desire to visit the water closet which was good and when I woke up the sheets were soaking with sweat. This was good I thought. My body is fighting whatever it is. I had another single bed next to me so I pushed Cameron Diaz over a little and snuggled in. Ah that's the dream version of the story. I slept well again and woke up at 7.30am feeling Camino better. My stomach said it was not feeling better three times before I left the room but my energy was there and I'd just go as far as I could. The goal being Villafranca del Bierzo which was about 25 km away.

I met up with everyone at a cafe and it was nice to see them. Their kindness in waiting a night and bringing food and water was incredible. A new girl from Germany, Lena, had joined us and we said goodbye to Chelsea from the U.S. who was waiting for her friend to arrive (I have since heard they are both now walking and on the way).

Soon we were walking out of the beautiful city of Ponferrada that I had not been able to look at properly the day before and my spirits were good. My toast and orange juice washed down with lovely fresh water was massaging my stomach just nicely.

We headed through the villages of Compostilla then Columbrainos and Fuentes Nuevas which, as always with every place, has its own character. There was one part of The Way that made me smile as it was a tunnel under houses and right under someone's bedroom. I wondered what it would be like for them in the summer when there are thousands passing through this each day.

The storks are free to build their huge nests anywhere and I found one amazing one right in the centre of town on top of a pole and the stork sat up there like it was his town. I gave him/

her a thank you and carried on. Now hungry, we entered the town of Camponaraya and it was a like a high street back home I thought. What was slightly different was that it had a vending machine in the middle that sold items such as orange juice, sex toys, lubricant, condoms etc. It was a classic Ann Summers type shop vending machine. Great idea I thought however I slowly turned my head to look back to see how far away the young priest was. Alexandro was smiling and all we had to do was wait, watch and go with the obvious banter that would follow. The priest arrived smiling knowing something was funny by our faces. The smallest of things can set you off laughing on the Camino. The priest looked and then looked again and looked at us then I played a kind of weird game of charades explaining to the future priest what was in the machine. Never thought I'd have to do that! When he twigged, there was much laughter and off we went to eat.

I was now hungry and as we sat at the bar I ordered and cheese and ham sandwich and a full fat Coke (it's good for the tummy someone said). When it arrived I was in toasty heaven. It was a normal toasty and the melted cheese melted more in my welcoming mouth. It was delicious and I washed it down with coke and thought of ordering another. I stopped and thought don't push it.

The sun was out and the weather warm. Remembering that one of my thoughts about being sick was possible heat or sun stroke I pulled out my floppy hat for the first time and was set to go. We were chatting and it was a normal day on the Camino. I was talking the Elea the theologian's wife and was asking what they were doing after the Camino and she told me they will visit Germany to see family then go back to Mexico. Asking what Alex was going to do, as his Appeal is at the Vatican in Rome, she said that it could take decades so basically you have to write that career off. My thoughts were of sadness that the church can just stop a seriously intelligent man from working because a senior member doesn't like to hear what someone has to say. Will it ever change? So all that knowledge and willingness to learn has meant that Professor Alexandro is now studying online in history and is wanting to specialise in Tibetan history and Buddhism. Incredible and I thought to myself I hope this guy gets everything he wants and deserves in life. He is a very kind, special, funny and incredibly smart guy. We carried on and I filled my water whenever I could and drank, drank, drank. Passing through the next town of Cacabelos I was happy that I was feeling better and we stopped at a little albergue to see if they sold food. They had nothing prepared but were lovely and offered us tea, coffee and fruit. I ate a very beautiful banana and remembered the advice I had been given by a friend about eating peel-able fruit like the explorers did. I was, after all being a bit of an explorer, so I did.

Again, we headed towards our goal and through beautiful countryside that was made up of many vineyards. I saw a dream home sitting on top of a hill under some trees. It was surrounded by its vineyards and I thought I could spend time there. A lot of time. A few kms later and we were entering Villafranca del Bierzo. I was happy that I had made the 25 km and while my feet were their usual aching self my stomach was growling less and less.

We booked in and I had a great shower. A hydro shower as Eduardo had seen this advertised and wanted to go so we all went. It was worth it. As I stood in this shower and jets of water stung and massaged my skin from all angles I wondered how I could persuade pops that this along with a whirlpool bath would be a great thing for our house. Eduardo had gone in search of food to cook and as I reflected on the day I was immensely happy to be back on the Camino. That thirty-six hours had been tough but the nineteen hours in a hotel were worth it. Life was back to great and more lessons learned.

Eduardo cooked again and it was delicious. Pasta with bacon and I don't know what the sauce was however it hit the spot. After dinner, there was a sofa and while Eduardo experienced the €2 foot massage I sat on the sofa and got chatting to a lovely Maltese girl Michelle who is on the Camino with her dad. We talked about the trips I had made to Malta and how I loved the place and we talked about the Camino and our stories. The time passed quickly and her dad was pleasant. 10.30pm came and we were sent to bed as it was lights out. People truly are amazing and my thoughts were with a friend who has taken on a huge task in life and changes. This walk makes you think. People help you along the way. Less than 200 km to Santiago now. My Camino Dream.

> *"Success is not final, failure is not fatal: it is the courage to continue that counts." ~ Winston Churchill*

# Day 29

## Just horsing around
## Villafranca del Bierzo to O'Cebreiro

As always, I couldn't get to sleep so lay and read and fell in and out of sleep throughout the night. I woke at one point by the sweat coming of me. It was pretty bad and my sheet at one side was wet. My body was obviously still fighting something so was happy with that and I balanced on the dry part of the bed. I woke up and had paid for breakfast, €2, which was amazing. I had cornflakes, toast and marmalade with a local sponge cake plus juice and coffee. It was a good start to the day and I bid farewell to the albergue cat and we all headed off towards a goal we were not so sure about as we had called ahead to see if we could do something that determined our ending position. The route would take us out of the town of Villafranca del Bierzo and start to head up and into another set of mountains. The gradual climb would be around 15km and the view through the valley back to the town was beautiful. Elea and I soon pushed off in front and we chatted. No matter how many times you speak with someone you always learn more and the time passed as tunnels and highways through the mountains appeared.

The first village we reached was Pereje and we stopped for a few minutes for a refreshment and loo break. Moving on and still climbing, the mountains on either side of us had alternative routes that you could take, however we had all decided that the main Camino route was good enough and we didn't require to add in extra mountains to it.

We were now around the village of Trabadelo and Eduardo and I reached there first so I ordered a coffee and a doughnut and waited for the others. They duly arrived and there is a lot of banter happening between everyone so after the usual bit of fun poked at each other my coffee was finished and I sat outside. I closed my eyes and listened to the running water of the mountain river. I vaguely remember some dreams and then the giggles as my picture was being taken. I don't know how long I'd napped for but it was brilliant. I was in a dream land.

I jumped up feeling refreshed and we set off again and my buddy this time was Lena. The new girl to our group. She is from Germany and is studying psychology. She's a lovely girl and we talked about why we are on the Camino and about our lives, what she is studying and her plans and timeline plus cultures and how they differ. She had volunteered in Romania for a while and that was interesting. We talked as we passed through three or four more small villages and while a lot were in disrepair I noticed that investment was happening and I assume this is due to the increase in pilgrims over recent years.

A lot of the Camino was now on the main road so care was taken when on these parts. We walked at different paces again and soon it was Eduardo and I that were ahead and he was saying how tired he was. The town we were heading to was in sight and some words of encouragement were given to him. We reached the village of Herrerias and that's where we confirmed the afternoon activity. We had booked to take the last stage of the climb using horses. This was a dream for me. We met Victor the owner who struck me as a really nice guy. One of those good looking younger Tom Jones types. The horses were ours so while they were prepared he phoned the local place to make sure we could get food. Off we went and the priest and Lena were there. They were not riding as the priest had done it before. The others went inside and it was a great little place. A family or friends were taking most of the place up with a lunch. It was also a bar and also the local store. We talked about how this little place would know everything that goes on in this tiny village. They prepared us meat, cheese, bread and tortilla and a drink which we all loved and it was a friendly little place. Paying up we gave our thanks to all and headed out to be immediately met with the sight of our four beautiful horses being groomed by Victor's wife and daughter. I had always dreamed of riding a horse and now it was going to come true and at such a special place and journey. Patience is indeed a virtue I thought. I was introduced to my beautiful girl Paulita and I said my hellos and apologies for eating excessively at times in my life however Paulita seemed to just look back and I swear she winked as if to say it's all ok. Just relax and enjoy. That's what I did. The four of us on horses and Victor walking we headed into the last section of the day. It was one of the most enjoyable experiences I've ever had riding a horse and I just felt at one with this beautiful creature and nature. The two hours passed in a flash and there was some conversation but mostly just looking at the view and enjoying the experience. After an hour or so we finally passed from the province of Leon to Galicia. A big milestone that signalled around 155 km to go. We reached the town O'Cebreiro and said goodbye to our beautiful horse friends. It had been majestic.

They say it always rains in Galicia and this stayed correct as three minutes after entering it started. It didn't matter though as I was over 4000ft again and it was beautiful. We booked in and as its Easter week and the only albergue its very busy so a different experience. We did however head to the church which is famous as it is said it's the place where a miracle happened. Long story short, not so good priest is holding a cup of wine and it turns to real blood. Priest now believes and becomes good priest. We went in and the chalice is still there in a cabinet that you can visit. It is an old church and really beautiful. An amazing day and a dream that will be repeated in the horse riding again. A day that ended yet again like nothing I had expected. Thank you St James.

"take every chance, drop every fear"~ Unknown

*A dream of riding a horse comes true*

# Day 30
## The wind can talk
## O'Cebreiro to Triacastela

It was very cold and after we ate our dinner last night I headed back to my sleeping bag and I didn't move from there other than to go to the bathroom. There were twenty-four pilgrims in this dorm from all different nations and one thing about the Camino is that you have to get used to living with a bunch of brand new people every day. Everyone tries to be as respectful as they can by making as little noise as they can and tip toeing about. I slept next to an old Spanish guy last night who started snoring and I "respectfully" whispered to him to stop. He did. People are up and about as early as 6am and that keeps going until around 8am. It can be quite funny as people who are trying to be quiet bump into things I have done this many times. An early morning comedy show of sorts however there were people going out the door of the room and leaving it open constantly and a cold draft was wrapping itself around my bunk every time so I would have to get up and close the door. I captured my frustration in these words.

## JUST SHUT IT

In and out you must go
It's use a must for you
Some are small and some are big
A place you must go through

There is a purpose for this thing
To name just but a few
To keep things out just like the cold
And yet you must go through

Designed to swing back and forth
On hinges that are true
They're made of wood and glass and stuff
These places you go through

The one small function that is a flaw
And something they don't do
They don't know how to close themselves
Right after you've passed through

They need your help and don't despair
As I need your help to
Every time you use a door
Just close it after you

It's not so hard and takes a tic

It's something you must do
Or I'll go mental have a fit
And chase right after you

I'll scream and shout are you just rude
Just bloody close the door
The cold got in and heat got out
Oh I just can't take no more

You'll smile and then apologise
and I'll shake to the core
And someone else will say calm down
It's just a wooden door

Agreed it's just a door I think
But there is one big but
The reason it has hinges on
Is so it can be shut

So please for mankind's sake
don't make our small heads sore
Be nice and smile when you pass through
And please just close the door

The albergues are getting busy and the town was small but touristy. "Roll up, roll up get your fridge magnet here" kind of stuff but in a really nice setting. I can't imagine what it would be like in high season when there can be thousands of people. Overall though a good sleep and we waited for everyone to leave before we got up. We were waiting for Tiger (the priest) and Lena who had stayed about 5 km away to catch up then the goal was to walk across the mountains and then down to Triacastela which was 20 km away. I was getting closer to Santiago and was ready to get there.

I looked out the window and said what a lovely view and I'm sure Eduardo swore in Italian as he looked out and saw nothing but mist and rain. It was forecast to be bad weather so out came the waterproofs and the poncho that was now held together by more yellow duct tape and we headed to the cafe to meet the others. A breakfast of toast and marmalade is common now and a nice start to the day. Rucksacks on and we were ready for the easy downhill 20km to our next stop.

It was raining as we left town and I looked down the valley to see where we would head as the Camino went straight and started to climb. I joked and said ah look we're heading up the mountain. The map had looked flat but the reality was we were going to do two summits today and I wasn't mentally ready. Mental adjustment change immediately and I was off climbing upwards as the rain started to get that little bit heavier but it was the noise of the wind that was getting my attention. It was getting louder like a prop engine plane was flying above and coming towards you slowly. Just this was a huge plane and much louder. The snow was on the roads and we climbed. As we turned into a different track Eduardo and I were laughing as the wind had just went from strong to pushing you about strong. Would my poncho hold out I thought?

We passed through the little village of Linares with its lovely church and onto our first summit where the Monumento do Peregrino stands at 1270m (4166 ft.). It's a beautiful monument and I'm sure the view is spectacular however on this occasion Eduardo and I were just trying to stay on two feet as the wind and rain of the Galician mountains tried its hardest to inflict any sort of discomfort it could. I remember thinking that we have layers of decent clothes on and yet thousands of people had done this in the past wearing only the clothes on their back. Maybe it was better and more waterproof as my stuff, while warm, was getting wet.

Heading downwards again we were heading to the town of Hospital de la Condesa where Natalie the American girl we had met a few days earlier was possibly going to be. I entered the small village and hoped she was there as I liked her. She had a good heart and this was the end of her Camino as she was having to go back to the place she lives and work with helping the teenage kids she looks after. I walked into the only cafe/bar in town and she was there so this became the first stop of the day. The others soon arrived and we chatted to Natalie as she was looking for a ride back to a place where she could get a bus to Ponferrada. As we talked a young Spanish couple with their baby said they would take her. Another one of my Camino friends said goodbye and as I gave her a hug I poked her eye with my finger. Way to go Iain I thought and just like that she was gone. That was four weeks to the day I had started walking and I thought about how many people I had met and how many I had said goodbye to. A few people now and all had been great. That's the Camino my German friend Luise used to say. I had heard from her telling me she would reach Santiago on Easter Sunday.

Two omelettes they were so insanely good I had to have a second and a coffee later and we were off again. It was nearly midday and we had only just walked over 5 km. The slowest day so far however it had been good.

The rain had eased off and we were in good spirits as we started climbing again. This was gradual until it suddenly kind of just seemed to go straight up. We were now going to Poio which was an altitude of 1335m (4380 ft.) and the climb up was tough but not long. The wind continued and the rain started again. It was head down and walk time and as there was a few km to the next town, which to be honest, I didn't know as it was too windy and wet to take things off to get to the guide book, so it was follow the arrow time.

What seemed to be a long time later we entered a town that

had a bar/cafe open and we were all soon inside its welcoming warm interior. I asked the owner where we were and I was pleased to learn that we were in Fonfria which meant we had walked 12 km and it was downhill from here. I undressed from my wet outer clothes and tucked into a wellliked pork and cheese sandwich that I washed down without guilt with a full fat Coke and double chocolate magnum. I thought of my friend who had warned me of the dangers of said indulgence however at 4000ft and in need of calories I was enjoying whatever. It was a delight and we all looked out of the window in a kind of shock and horror as the rain decided to increase in volume and together with its friend the gale force wind it was playing the raining horizontal game.

Brave faces on and we all set off. The weather was tough and it was really head down time. No pictures were taken for quite a while and I had seen Eduardo run past me and into the distance screaming he was soaking wet. I wondered if I'd ever see him again and not long after the German girl Lena caught up with me. She had walked an extra 5k uphill to meet us today and her poncho was ripped and she was soaking. The wind was so strong that I shouted to come away from a steep edge for fear that she would get blown over. As I held onto my head covers and she walked on I shouted to her to look into the distance as the town was there but I don't think she heard and she was gone in a cold and wet flash. I passed through a snow drift that was taller than me and I thought about how people try and do this in the winter. Insane but they do. I soon came below the cloud line and everything started to ease off and I passed through the town of Filloval and through a herd of cows, slowly making their way up to the not so nice weather, helped by the farm dog ensuring they went the correct way. Their eyes I'm sure were sad at the hard climb and black clouds that lay ahead but on they continued. Funny how in life we can see black clouds and a struggle ahead but we keep on going I thought. Who were the dogs barking and moving us along when we do? I thought about the times that I had done that as I was not brave enough to make a change. I knew I was now.

The rain had stopped and I turned a corner to see the Italian borrowing some chord that he was excited to explain to me he could use as a washing line. He was happy and we both talked about the crazy weather and how it felt to be coming into town. As we entered we did laugh at being the only two people in the street on a Saturday evening. Time for the albergue.

We checked into the albergue and we had a room for four which is rare but even rarer we had a single bed. No one above moving about all the time. Luxury. I headed to see where the showers were and as I looked in shock I called on Eduardo to come quickly. He arrived at the scene and just said in his Italian accent "I can't believe it." We jumped around hugging like little kids who had won the egg and spoon race. We had a bath in the albergue. I was first in and spent a luxury thirty minutes and emptied it and started running another one for my Italian friend. I came out and bless him he was standing there with his towel waiting he was that excited. A great end to a tough 20 km.

I put my clothes in for washing as they were wet which left me a jumper and boxer shorts so no going out for dinner. I said I would cook and the troops went for the stuff and I cooked up a storm wearing my boxers and jumper in the community kitchen as some ate and others watched. It was just another great night after a challenging but worth every-second type of day.

*"Sunshine is delicious, rain is refreshing, wind braces us up, snow is exhilarating; there is really no such thing as bad weather,*

*A windy Monumento do Peregrino*

# Day 31

## The Irish are here
## Triacastela to Sarria

As I went to bed, I gave a Spanish good evening to the locals who were having a party of sorts in the albergue and pushed the chair in and hit the top of my left foot of the wood. Instant pain and I hobbled up to bed wondering how so much pain could come from a mere tap of the foot. I went to bed and hoped that by morning it would not hurt.

A night of not too bad a sleep I thought although I awoke a few times as usual however my bed was soooo squeaky that the slightest movement made a fanfare of noise to others in the vicinity. When I woke up and looked at the time it was 8.21am. OMG I thought what a sleep. I've never slept that late when I realised that it was my phone on British time and the clocks had gone forward. The others said no it's 7.21am. Then we all thought it might be 8.21 and I checked the Internet. The time had indeed gone forward. Now we knew where we stood we got up and started the packing routine. Another thing you have to get used to on the Camino is you unpack and pack every day and night, you wash clothes (or get someone to do it for you wink) every day. It's part of the routine. Does it get easier and fun? No. There is nothing fun for me in packing and I have it down to an efficient small piece of time. It's just part of it.

One thing that had disturbed me a little was that Elea had said I was snoring and that she was going to move to another place but there was none. She moved my bed and I turned over and stopped. On more enquiry, it was seemingly a very good snore and I have now told everyone in the group that on the very odd occasion I do then to just shake me. It also let me know that at least one part of the night I slept well.

My foot was extremely sore from where I had hit it the night before and I was kind of scared to put my boots on as I knew they would tighten across the painful area. I'm not going to lie but the slightest pain in my foot and I was making plans of how I could walk without boots and all sorts of things. I was going to Santiago no matter what. A sandal with sock and a plastic bag to keep the foot dry was all in plan. Pain cream rubbed in and painkillers taken and the boots were on. It was sore but off we set. I thought if it gets too painful then I'll stop but the goal was only 19 km to the town of Sarria.

I had noticed on the guide the start of the day was a walk up a hill and I thought oh that's great it's only a few hundred metres of a climb however when I worked it out in feet it was over 1000ft. I quite liked the thought of an early morning climb. Moving out of the town it threatened to rain and my rain gear was on and I was concentrating on my foot. Half a kilometre and the pain was going and then gone. Either the painkillers were kicking in or the movement was helping. It didn't hurt for the rest of the day so I was amazingly relieved and pleased. The countryside of Galicia is green and fertile. The mountains provide their own micro climate and I had to remember that I was starting at around 2000ft and going to around 3000ft so as Eduardo and I started the climb up through the narrow valley we passed waterfalls and streams that were just beautiful, a small village that had no one there other than the chickens and cocks strutting about singing their early morning cock-a-doodle-doos. It was quite peaceful. The hill got steeper and I moved on ahead of Eduardo and passed a giant shell painting on the hillside that looked like an attempt to make a nice resting place that had been left to fall away. I hoped someone would give it a quick clean up as it was a pretty place. A while later I reached the top of the hill and the view was breathtaking. I stood for a while just to take it in and it felt good to have climbed it with not a bit of pain from my foot. The cold air was nipping my ears and cheeks but it was fresh and crisp as it passed through my nose on its cleansing mission to my lungs.

It was off downhill now and I could see the town of Sarria in the distance and my stomach was saying a little something in it would be good. We reached the tiny village of Fruela and I had an omelette with coffee and a chocolate ice cream lolly. All were delicious and we were all back together. We set off down the hill again and the conversation was about foods that shock us. We were told how in some places in China it's expensive but people eat monkey brains while the animal is still alive. The priest talked about the whole eating dog thing in Korea and how it is rude to say no if someone offers you it. He said that it tastes nice. He no longer wants to eat it though and talked about the way views are changing. We soon turned a corner and ran into the cutest puppy ever and that was the end of that conversation. After some time of playing with the most adorable pup on the planet we headed off again with lots of chat. We walk and talk about lots of things. I can never remember everything till I really reflect but it's fun.

We passed through the last tiny village of Aguiada. What I loved about this place was the smallest church just waiting there and when you look inside it was quite beautiful. A handful of people must use it to pray.

We were not far from our goal and I was telling funny stories when I heard the lovely voice of an Irish girl. This is when I met Ciara and Aodan from Dublin. We got chatting and we walked together with their friend Coo the Korean all the way into the town. They are a lovely couple and Ciara is hilarious and I was chuckling away at the stories she was telling as we walked into town. Aodan was asking locals where we were as we had been chatting and went off route and we were soon back on route towards our rendezvous point. It was nice to meet some new

Camino friends. We found the albergue and the others were already there and the Irish and Korean decided to stay also. The showers were good and after a bite to eat I had a quick walk around and came back to the albergue where I drank some non-alcoholic beer with my new Irish friends around a most amazing fire.

As we sat around the fire another Irish lady arrived and started chatting. She had just been for an "amazing massage" so my new friend Ciara the Irish girl and I both were wanting to know where and how much. We would both have one and I'd head there first as she was going for dinner with her man. She decided to come with me though to book a spot and we headed off to where we both assumed the place was and realised upon arrival that we had not brought the map. Ciara went into a bar to ask how to get a massage. There was a few strange looks at her and it did look a bit dodgy. I helped by standing far enough away that I could laugh my head off at her misfortune at the situation. We established where to go and arrived. It was a courtyard with a cover and some sheets around the table. The lady came out and explained there was only enough time for one person and it had to be back or legs and not both. Ciara looked at me and I could see the "I hate you" well up in her eyes as I knew she had to go to dinner. Feeling guilty for at least two seconds I said that I would take the slot and I laughed as Ciara said I hate you and sprinted up the stairs. I decided then that I'd lie to her and say it was a rubbish massage either way. She would know or assume I was not telling the truth which would make the situation funnier. As I waited I was startled by a chap on the window a few minutes later. It was Ciara pointing at me and saying something and laughing. She was with the others and going for dinner and I'm sure she was saying "enjoy your massage Iain I'm so happy for you."

I went in and the lady worked on my legs and feet for twentyfive minutes and I have to say it felt good and it cost a mere

€10. I returned to the albergue where we chatted and eventually headed to bed where I lay and watched some Still Game and the History of Buddhism which was interesting.

Life again was good and we were all a day closer to Santiago. It was getting closer and my excitement was growing.

> "The great thing about new friends is that they bring new energy to your soul." ~ Shanna Rodriguez

# Day 32
## New friends that inspire
## Sarria to Portomarin

aking up we all got ready and the forecast was rain for the day so all the clothes were on and we had a coffee and pastry in the cafe next door as we waited for Chelsea and her friend, the girl who was at Brussels airport, who were catching up with us. Info came back and forth as to where they were and the others, namely Alex and Elea after smooching and dressing weird, decided to head on and Eduardo and I waited for the girls.

A while later we heard from Chelsea to say her and Madii were not far away and before we knew it they were right there and both with smiles. They had done well over the previous couple of days to catch up with us and poor Chelsea was starting to sport blisters. After introductions to Madii the four of us headed up the street and past the castle to head to our goal for the day which was 23 km away and the town of Portomarin.

The road today would see us climb over a 1000ft again out of the town and it was all beautiful rolling hills and farms. While it was raining, the chat kept us busy and I was getting to know Madii.

Madii was walking into Brussels airport as the people were running out after the bombs. Literally minutes had separated her from inside. We walked and I listened to her story. It is an incredible story and I hung on every word and my mind tried to visualise the words she was saying. She talked of never seeing people come together like that before and help, how they were all taken from the airport and the nervousness of wondering where they were going "where were they being taken" as they were not being told. Once safe, then her epic journey to get to Amsterdam airport and still ensure family and friends knew everything was ok. From there to Madrid and then to Ponderal to meet Chelsea and here she was five days later walking next to me smiling and excited about life and telling this incredible story. I couldn't help but admire her get on with it attitude and I also thought that the Camino may just have a way of doing its own thing to make things in life just be ok.

The first village we walked through saw a "Del Boy" type character lure us into his quite lovely barn conversion souvenir shop with the "I stamp your credential". He did and we all had another stamp to prove at the end we had passed through the Camino. It was getting more touristy as this part of the Camino is the part you must do if you want your certificate which is the last 100km. It is a bit more from Sarria, where we left that day, however where many pilgrims leave from to complete the last 100km.

On our way out, we passed the church and a little old man was on the road and motioned us to go look at the church. I think that St James is telling me something when things like that happen and we followed the old fellow down to the church wondering what it was about. The church was not the normal looking Spanish type and the old guy told us that it was a Romanesque style and was over nine hundred years old. I loved the inside and for the first time saw the memorials outside for this part of Spain. He was happy to give us a stamp and I left a donation in their box. I love stops like that. Unexpected and mind blowing.

We kept on walking over burns and through lush green woodland and passing through farm after farm. I laughed as I never in my life thought I'd see a Lamborghini driving through the gates of a farm covered in cow shit and dogs running around it barking. The old farmer in his Wellington boots got out of the machine that sounded impressive and laughed as I exclaimed "Lamborghini" and snapped a picture. Another Camino first. A Lamborghini tractor.

We were hungry and wet so it was a welcoming sight to see the cafe/bar. I ordered lunch and soon the others came in and we all sat and chatted. I saw other pilgrims I had seen over the previous week and said hi and for the first time phoned ahead to book an albergue as a couple we had tried had been sold out. Lena the German girl had very sore feet and had decided to stop at the next albergue a km away to rest which was sensible and Tiger said he'd also stay which was good so she had someone from the group.

The rest of us headed and as we passed through a town or two I listened to stories from the girls and looked out for the marker that said less than 100km to Santiago. It was a bit of a significant symbol after walking nearly 700km already. We took our pictures and I couldn't help but have a bit of a proud of myself smile on my face. I had to make sure I got there on Friday and then I could really be proud. As we started to descend we were going through some heavy mud when we ran into the couple who are doing the Camino with their wee one. I had heard about them as news travels on the Camino and they were lovely and their daughter sat in her push buggy smiling and laughing at all of us going past. We offered to help but carrying the wee one is their job so Eduardo took their rucksack for a while till we got out of the mud. They had also started in St Jean and I loved their attitude and positivity. They still arrived at the same time as us as I followed them over the bridge into town.

We passed through more villages on the way down and stopped for a Magnum Double Choc ice creams that I treated the girls to and we talked about dreams and what theirs were and it was good. Alex and Elea were behind us and Eduardo had headed off in front. The afternoon had been dry and the chat good as the town came into view.

We reached the town around 5pm and it was nice that Alexandro had booked the albergue as there was no stress. Poor Chelsea was not so great with blisters that were hurting and we headed to the albergue that was nice to settle in for the night. The albergue was modern and clean and the girls set off to the pharmacy as the blisters Chelsea has are pretty bad.

I went for a shower and, as I do a lot of thinking in the shower, it was there in a flash the whole reason for my Camino flooded my mind and in a minute or two a poem had formed. It all just suddenly made sense and the warm water was soothing as it splashed on my skin and the words in my head flowed over my brain and out of my mouth. I was content.

A poem about The Way by Iain McKie

### THE WAY

*The question why had been asked*
*As why I walked The Way*
*I didn't know the reason why*
*I didn't know what to say*

*The days rolled by and miles I clocked*
*The questions they did come*
*Why are you walking all this way?*
*Was I just being dumb*

Up mountains high and through the rain
More people and we would talk
And that one question I would ask
Why are you doing this walk

More answers, of different ways
Some sporting some more deep
All were personal and all were theirs
And all were quite unique

A loss I heard and change of life
To find themselves they sought
To escape the race and just relax
Why am I hear I thought?

Then in a shower and out the blue
The reason I was smart
This journey was not coming to an end
This really was just the start

The way with all its ups and downs
Was just a map of life
The pain i'd felt along the way
Was payback for the strife

The rainy days were just a test
To show me all can change
With sun and snow around the bend

*That life can be so strange*

*The people taught me how to smile*
*Be patient and forgive*
*All this combined I had to scream*
*The Ways taught me how to live*

*So, on I'll walk into this life*
*With soul and mind awake*
*The reason that I came this way*
*Is to see the life I'll make*

*To love and help and make things fun*
*To live out every day*
*To treat myself more kindly now*
*I'm glad I've walked "The Way"*

I went for dinner on my own and looked at the church which was interesting as it had been moved to its current location brick by brick after the valley where it originally sat had been flooded due to the building of a dam. Another day of meeting new people, learning more about my friends and enjoying what the Camino offers. Beauty and intrigue and time for your brain to relax. Four days I'll be in Santiago I thought. That was making me think a lot.

"Man cannot discover new oceans unless he has the courage to lose sight of the shore." —André Gide.

*Alexandro and his wife Elea celebrate the 100km marker with a kiss*

# Day 33

## Performing surgery is all part of it
## Portomarin to Palas De Rei

I had gone for dinner myself last night as I craved pizza and when it arrived it was a poor version of the frozen ones you buy and as my wee mum used to say, "hunger's good kitchen" and never a truer word as I scoffed it down promising myself to treat myself to a proper and delicious pizza as soon as I could. As I walked back to the albergue I decided I'd buy the group a chocolate ice cream each and stopped off to purchase some treats and I was looking forward to sitting back and enjoying the chocolate deliciousness. I have seemed to have grown a fondness to this type of treat on a daily basis and insist others join in. Maybe that's to make me feel less guilty or it's possibly just because I like to see the smiles on people as they tuck in.

When I came back USA times two were sitting with Eduardo finishing what they had made and Chelsea was looking to pop her blisters and treat them. Her feet were in a mess and it seemed like she needed help. Minutes later the surgery was set up and as I was about to saw off her foot when nurse Madii handed me the syringe to pop blister number one. Chelsea freaked out as she was not liking this and I took her foot and made the tiny incision and I drained the three blisters one after the other and then they were covered with stuff from the pharmacy and then Compeed applied and then strips. The funny thing about blisters is there is a limitless supply of advice on what to do and what not to do. My aim was to keep them from getting infected. Chelsea laughed hard and seemingly this is a normal reaction for her when in pain. She laughs at my jokes a lot I thought! Surgery complete, we all went to bed and the mattress was a comfy one. I left instructions that my nose was blocked so if I snored to give me a shove. Well no one did and I had a great sleep in terms of Camino sleeps.

We were the last again to leave the albergue and Chelsea's feet were ok so we set off. Eduardo was still in the albergue on the phone so he would catch up. The weather was wet so with rain gear on and my poncho sporting great yellow duct tape we headed for another climb of over a 1000ft. We're up and down hills all the time. As I walked out of town the view was beautiful with steep slopes that held on precariously to their small private vineyards and homes looking over the river and lake below. I strode on up the hill which five weeks ago would have had me stopping for breath every twenty paces but I now actually enjoy the exercise up these hills. I made a note to not be enjoying it so much when I'm back home. I laughed to myself at my own jokes.

One of the biggest things about the Camino is that I did not know what to expect scenery wise but the little I did imagine or saw on TV had been nothing like it actually is. I've passed through many regions and all with their own unique countryside. It's been beautiful and sometimes more like home than home looks. I walked with a girl from London briefly who was making me laugh a lot as she was talking about the fields and grass and that she could get that near home. She was funny complaining and while she was right you can get this at home I couldn't help but think I was enjoying everything about it and it was all brand new. I loved it. We passed markers that people just build if there is a slight chance a yellow arrow is not nearby. I love that people realise this and take the time to point others on the way. It's the way the Camino is. People just help people. There is a common bond no matter what your reason for walking is.

We passed a beautiful field of green grass and the U.S. had talked about how they loved to "frolic" in such fields. We stopped and they went frolicking and dancing. Crazy Yanks I thought but it was fun to see them all smiles.

I was keeping an eye towards the back of the group as Alexandro had a sore hip that has slowed him down and I was quite prepared to stop for the day if he needed, however, he is not one for complaining and walked through pain and slowly kept going.

We stopped for a bite to eat and I had a full-on pork chop with chips and eggs. I was hungry and as I ate we watched as the heavens opened and I realised the poncho, while held together with tape, would get good use today. We headed off again and climbing more we passed through a couple of small villages. Most buildings that we passed were in some way farm related and I spoke cow often as we passed the lovely animals. A pilgrim with his dog passed us. I had seen him a few days earlier and the dog was always so happy dancing along the trail saying hello to others and carrying his own doggy rucksack. The view again was beautiful and being a huge farming area, I was not surprised to run into the local tractor sales area and I had a look at all the tractors available. I have always enjoyed tractors since I can remember and being on the farm on my holidays when I was young was always fun. Maybe I just needed a little croft with a highland coo or two and a tractor. A small B&B to help people enjoy wherever it was I was living with my tractor and coos.

While Paris in a Ferrari had been fun (I was there last year) I thought that a trip round the countryside in a tractor is a far better experience.

My feet were hurting now and I was walking with Alexandro as his wife Elea went ahead with the girls. I always enjoy my chats with Alexandro. He is just a fountain of knowledge and I laugh to myself sometimes thinking he must be bored with my continuous questions on history, religion and so on. He always answers and gives explanation. I've learned a lot from him. Most of all I've laughed with him and made a good friend.

We passed through some more farming villages and stopped at a cafe/bar. The feeling was good as I thought we still had about 10k to go and it was pointed out we were only 5.5km away. To celebrate I had apple pie. It was delicious however the owner looked at me as if I was stupid when I asked for cream. I may have insulted the cook so smiled and ate. It was delicious though.

We passed through another village and the graves in this region are again like boxes stacked on top of each other. I thought I'd need to try and find out the reason why they bury people like this. We passed over the hill and it was all downhill to the town. I had walked on my own for a while and enjoyed the operatic voices punching my ear drums with their booming noise.

The rain didn't let up and we were all soon in the town of Palas de Rei. 25km and the last 10k had hurt but I knew Santiago was now only three days walk away. I settled in and went to buy a Pizza. There was a Pizzeria in town. Upon arrival, I met one of the German girls I know and she told me she had been waiting for an hour and I thought there is no pizza that good when I'm hungry so off I set to eat at a restaurant. It was nice and I ate a hamburger. I had to get over my fear that it would make me sick again and I'm confident this one won't.

It had been a wet day but I don't think you feel the rain or see it as there is too much going on around and in your head to care. Well that's how I think. It had been another great day and I'd be lying if I said I wasn't looking forward to Santiago. This journey never stops amazing me.

"Life is a journey, not a destination." ~ Ralph Waldo Emerson

*My great friend Mr Italy, Eduardo*

# Day 34

## Octopussy is a new one
## Palas de Rei to Ribadiso de Baixo

I spent the last hours of the evening chatting to my Maltese friend Michelle and Eduardo while doing my daily painting. I find that quite relaxing at the end of the day. I went to bed with the intention of watching something as we had Wi-Fi however I couldn't find my earphones. My other pair I had stood on during the day so were a gift to the Camino gods and now I couldn't find the spare set. I had them when I arrived so Alexandro let me borrow his as I would find mine in the morning. I have still not found them and have also lost my poncho that has duct tape all over it. Both items I was wearing when I arrived. The Camino Gods now possess them and I have faith no rain will fall on me for the next few days. I put on a programme about the solar system and can't even remember the starting part of it so must have been out like a light as they say. I must have been conscious of snoring as I caught myself a couple of times and rolled over. The sleep was good and in the morning, I got the all clear that I had not snored however it turned out Chelsea had. I laughed at this scenario.

We were once again the last to leave and we toddled over to the church opposite for a look around. It was a simple but pretty place and we stamped out credentials to prove we had been there and headed on out of town as the goal was 26km today and a couple of people were hurting so we would stop earlier if required.

Walking out of Palas de Rei we passed a couple of lovely monuments which we were chatting about when the countryside soon opened up again to green fields while the Camino followed forest paths. The weather was dry and I knew the Camino Gods were happy to keep it that way for me as I had given my poncho to them. The paths had some wet parts however we navigated our way through and it was not long before we arrived one by one at our first stop for coffee and doughnuts in the small hamlet called Casanova. I loved the name and we sat there and waited for Madii as she was a bit slower due to a foot injury. We have agreed that we are the laziest group on the Camino as we are now starting to take stops a lot and really taking it easy or is it that we are the most sensible group on the Camino and enjoying ourselves.

Off we set on our next leg towards the larger town of Melide which was about 8 km away. The rain clouds were black in the distance but the gods were blowing the wind from behind us and I knew we were ok. Eduardo and I were way off in front and as always, the two of us discussed the important things in life and laughed a lot. He talked as usual of his girl and how he couldn't wait to see her. The time just passes when you're with Eduardo and we laughed a lot as we passed through more lushes' green towards the town.

Just outside the main town there was a guy who was doing a wax stamp for your credential. It was for a donation but I saw he had a prosthetic leg and the background garage showed weights and other fitness equipment. We chatted to him and it turns out he represents Spain at the Paralympics in discus, shot and javelin. He was a nice guy and talked to Eduardo about going to Italy soon for a big competition.

It wasn't long before we were in Furelos which is a small beautiful village on the outskirts of Melide. The bridge in was in such a perfect setting and we stopped in at the church to have a look. The stamp showed Jesus on the cross however with one arm not nailed but hanging to the side. I'd never seen this before and saw that they had a statue on the wall the same. I wondered if there was any significance and would try and find out. It wasn't long before Chelsea arrived and then sooner than I thought Alexandro and Elea, Alexandro being a trooper with his sore hip, we decided that we would have a stop and eat and wait for Madii. She arrived quicker than I thought and soon we were all relaxing and chatting away. We were not half way and it was into the afternoon. It was relaxing though.

There had been a text from the priest, who we had not seen in a couple of days, because he and Lena had stopped early one day due to Lena having sore feet. They were not far behind and were walking fast to catch up. I made the joke about the pace that we were going that someone starting in Pamplona would catch up but that was ok. Santiago was not going anywhere and then I heard Eduardo say the priest is coming over the bridge. I jumped up and sure enough there was the priest and Lena coming over the bridge. It was great to see them and we were all soon hugging like old friends who had not seen each other in years. The Camino can really build friendships. With jokes and smiles we headed to Melide with one thing to do and that was stop at a place so Elea could eat octopus. Fifteen minutes later and we were stopped again. Three people went in and the rest of us stayed outside the octopussy restaurant. I could see through the window the rather big creatures being dropped into boiling water then, I presumed cooked, and being cut up with a pair of regular scissors to be served. About 20 minutes later I decided to go in and see how things were going. Elea invited me to try a piece of octopussy, so I did and it was ok. Not much taste and a wee bit slimy maybe. At least I had tried it I thought. No need to try again though.

It was time to push on and as we left the town I couldn't help but say that it seemed a bit of poor town. I was maybe wrong but it seemed like it could use a hand. It was cool though that between houses there was a flock of sheep and then between more a crop. Not something you see every day. We were in the country again and the priest, Eduardo and I talked guy stuff and we laughed a lot. The priest commented on how he had had lovely deep conversations with Lena and now this chat with us. It was hilarious as Eduardo explained to the priest what "the magic hole" was in Italy. I thought I was going to die.

A while later we reached the small village of Bonete and it was time for another stop. We waited for everyone to arrive so we could decide what to do. It was now after 4pm and it was important everyone was still fit to walk if we were going forward. Tired hips and sore feet did not stop this lot and we set off for the last 6km to where we would stay. As we walked up and down what we're very steep hills I remember thinking of how Alexandro had said it was flat all the way now. We were all spread out with heads down and walking hard as this was no flat surface. It was tough. An hour or so later I was coming down the hill into Ribadiso de Baixo. As I reached the albergue I smiled. The Camino gods let it start to rain as I pushed the handle to enter. I knew they were looking after me. All I had to do was give them a gift. A shower later and I headed out for dinner myself. I couldn't resist the Galician steak followed by chocolate mousse. I deserved a treat and so I sat and treated myself. A day about people and friends reunited, of excitement that it's just 41 km to Santiago, grateful that everyone is still fit and happy just to be alive and on the Camino.

"Plenty of people miss their share of happiness, not because they never found it, but because they didn't stop to enjoy it." ~ William Feather

*My Maltese friends Michelle and her dad David*

# Day 35

## Santiago eve — Amazing
## Ribadiso de Baixo to Pedrouzo

The remainder of the evening was lovely and I chatted with Malta Michelle and the others then Eduardo and I used the leg and foot massager. It was divine and I tried to think of who I can get an hour massage from at home as I'm going to treat myself. It was getting late and everyone retired and while it was a modern albergue it was cold and I had two blankets on top of my sleeping bag. I eventually was drifting off to music however there was a low drone from a snorer and it was creeping into my ears over my music. I took my earphones (that I've borrowed) out to locate said snorer and was not unsurprised to hear it was Chelsea who was snoring away and as it continued for a while I got up and shook her bed and said you are snoring. She remembered in the morning and we laughed. When she stopped the guy at the other side of me started. Another night on the Camino and my thoughts of developing a snoring app so I can sleep to the sounds of the Camino when I get home.

This morning I didn't want to wait about so when I was ready I set off and even then it was still nearly 9. I had told the others I would either see them on the way or at the destination. It was a nice crisp morning and I was happy at getting on the road. I walked the first couple of km to the town of Arzua having a chat to pops. It was good to talk about where I was and all things Camino. I stopped to have a little bit of breakfast and as I was paying young Madii popped her head through the door to say hi so we set off together. It was still a nice morning and I was confident that the Camino gods would not let rain fall on me till after I have arrived in Santiago. Madii and I walked and talked. She is doing great considering having a sore foot but has just kept going. We talked about some stuff and she told me about her life and how it's made her the person she is. I walked and listened intently to this young girl's amazing story and I thought "courage". She has a zest for life and her dreams are great. The Camino is a great place where you can just talk and I enjoyed this time with Madii. We were soon approaching a stop and it was time for anything really to go in my stomach.

We stopped at a lovely cafe and we shared an insanely delicious pastry when, with delight, Madii shouted "there's Chelsea" and sure enough my other American friend arrived with her usual own way of making us smile. We all ate and chatted before the three of us set off again on the trail. The two of them are funny together and we were soon talking about movies and what our favourites were and why, what were good documentaries and conspiracy theory and all that goes with that and I took note of a couple of movies and docs they raved about as we passed slowly through the beautiful Spanish countryside and small villages. The Way was marked but I had managed to miss some arrows but the girls lead the way through some narrow places. Chelsea's blisters were not hurting which was a relief for Dr McKie. Job done I thought as we talked and talked. We soon passed the less than 30km to go marker and it was hard to comprehend that we were that close to Santiago. It was not long before another stop came into view and I asked the girls if they wanted a beer. I went inside to order and took one look at the place. The dancing, drums and positive vibe made me turn around and say y'all may want to come in. The bar was very cool with people really having a good time and soon Chelsea had a bongo drum between her legs and she was bagging away on it. Madii acquired a guitar and another Camino moment took shape. The guitar was plucked, the drum beats hypnotic rhythm pulled the people closer and Madii sang. This girl has an amazing voice and I was sitting there happy that I was alive as people danced and clapped to these two youngsters impromptu display of musical talent. One word I thought, just one word "Amazing" I was in Camino heaven as I just watched my friends have so much fun and the people dance.

We left the bar on a high and started walking with more and more great conversation. An American guy Ron passed and I walked with him. A nice guy from San Francisco who is a teacher and we had a great conversation about politics and other relevant stuff. A few kms later we reached a bar and Ron headed off and I went inside to wait for the girls. As I drank my coffee, the confirmation not that I required it – that the Camino gods were not letting it rain on me was confirmed as it rained hard and the girls and I sat and watched. When my omelette was finished, the sun came out and we left the bar.

As we left a familiar face was standing at the other side of the street smiling. The Italian was ready to talk and Eduardo and I set off for the finish and as usual the conversation had us both pissing ourselves laughing. We walked through the tree lined path and it was not long till we entered the town and we were both talking about how our feet were sore. We waited for the girls and headed to the albergue where we had arranged to meet everyone. We were looking forward to it as it advertised having a sauna and we were all up for it. "I'm sorry we are full" the lady said to us. I didn't panic as I have faith in the Camino and she said we have a brand new albergue that's only been open a week that has beds. We walked the five hundred metres to the other place and we landed in albergue heaven. The albergue name is O Triquetral. Brand new mattresses with a modern living room with sofas and a kitchen. The hydro showers were roasting hot and the others were soon to arrive. How on earth could today get any better.

Sandrux, a Spanish girl we had met on The Way, arrived and was in with us. I had left to go for a quick snack and Sandrux came into the same place so we sat in the sun for a while and talked about life of and what our countries were doing with independence. It was a nice time and we sneakily shared some pizza before heading back to the albergue for dinner that the priest and Eduardo were preparing.

We all sat and ate some great food and laughed a lot. There was talk of how the Camino was coming to an end and where we would be going to stay tomorrow and, of course, there was many laughs.

Thank you, St James, for delivering another amazing day with amazing people. Tomorrow I will come Santiago and visit you in person to say thank you.

> "Be yourself, accept yourself, value yourself, forgive yourself, bless yourself, express yourself, trust yourself, love yourself, empower yourself." ~ Unknown

# Day 36

## Santiago and thank you St. James
## Pedrouzo to Santiago de Compostela

Today was not going to be like any other day on the Camino I thought as I tossed and turned in my ever so comfy bunk bed. I was wondering what it would feel like to arrive in Santiago. The music and documentaries I was playing did not help me get to sleep however eventually the days walking took over and I was to awaken around 7am and some were up and about. All I said to them was "Santiago".

I looked outside and it was still dark and I could tell it was cold. I packed all my things and everyone started heading off when they were ready. First the U.S. girls and then the priest and then Lena. The theologist and his wife were next and then it was Mr Italy and myself. Sandrux, our newest member would walk on after us.

After a few kms our natural pace separated us and I was on my own walking at a decent pace. I, for some reason, had a lot of energy and I was passing through forests and open fields as the morning sun seemed to be that little bit more beautiful today. Everything seemed that little bit more beautiful. I was messaging pops to say where I was and that I was heading to Santiago when he sent me a message to say that I should be proud of myself as he was proud. It was just after 8am and my first joyful tears of the day were blurring out the crisp picture of the fields in front of me. I stopped for a moment to just take the air and day in. I said thanks to St James again and moved on.

The walk, while looking fairly flat in the guide book, offered its usual steep parts and I was loving it. I can fly up these hills now and was soon passing newly started pilgrims with a Buen Camino and a smile. Before I knew it, I could hear the noise of jet engines as the airport came close. I knew that I had covered the ground quickly but when I saw a 12.5 km to Santiago marker I couldn't believe it. The Camino and my mind were obviously working hard and I soon caught up with the priest and Lena and then Madii.

The Way was busy with school kids at this point and again I moved in through a small village and stopped at a cafe to stamp my credential. It was only after 11am now and another cafe came up so I thought stop or you'll be in Santiago by mid-day. I sat with music playing and the sun beating of my face when the others started to arrive. Usually we just say hello with a smile but this time there were hugs going on. Real excitement to see others and laughs. After twenty minutes or so the whole crew was there including Michelle and her dad from Malta. I was happy to see them also and I got to try Maltese food. Cheesy snacks. They were lovely. What a great stop and after we were all fed and watered we again set off at our own pace. The next stop would be Santiago I thought.

The next village I passed through was Monte del Gozo which overlooks Santiago. A great monument sits proudly at its highest point and this translation of the name is "very happy" as this is where in the olden days pilgrims would see the spires of the cathedral for the first time and break down crying in happiness. I looked but did not see the cathedral however right there, a stone's through away it seemed, was Santiago de Compostela. The place I'd been walking towards for five weeks.

I was soon walking through the outer parts of the city. I was on my own and could see Eduardo and Chelsea up ahead. I had had a few moist eye moments along the way that day but I couldn't feel anything. My mind was full of thoughts and I couldn't separate them except one. Look for the cathedral. I was here to say hello to St James. The modern streets of this large town eventually give way to the older part of town. I had passed Eduardo and Chelsea at this point and then as I crossed over a street I saw the spires of the cathedral for the first time and they were close. My heart was beating a little harder and I wasn't seeing the yellow arrows now. I was just walking towards those spires. As I passed the fountain I knew I was not far away but I could not see it. I walked down a narrow road and then I heard that magical word "aqui, aqui" and there he was. Thomas my Swedish friend standing in the middle of the street and he had been waiting. It was so amazing to see him and we hugged. With little time wasted he was walking with me and the cathedral was right there. Well one side and we moved quickly towards the tunnel that would take me to the main plaza. A girl was playing the Galician pipes which are the same as bagpipes by the looks of it but I had no time to stop.

Then I was there. Standing in front of the cathedral in front of the main plaza. I know Thomas was saying things but I really didn't hear. My mind was taking it all in. I couldn't believe I was there and it seemed like it was always meant to be. That moment was bliss. My emotions were high and I was tearing up. Thomas took pictures and then Eduardo arrived to hugs as did Chelsea. I took a few minutes to myself and walked across the square to call pops. A call I enjoyed making and I couldn't speak for the first minute due to the emotion. It was fantastic to say dad I'm here and I have done it. He was so happy for me and then I got to say hi to my great friend Junie who was having coffee with him. The release of the tension now left my body and I was so happy.

It wasn't long before our whole team was there. The Australians arrived and the Irish too. We were seeing people all over the place that we had met on the Camino. It was amazing. A bunch of strangers all sharing a special time of their lives.

We headed to the albergue and checked in then it was straight off to collect our Compostela. A certificate that shows you have walked the Camino and you prove this with all the stamps you collect on the way. This was another good feeling.

Now it was time for the important part of the walk. It was time for me to go and visit St James. I wanted to thank him personally. We entered the cathedral through a special door that is only opened in holy years and I believe that it can help get rid of your sin. As I passed through I made the point that to remove all my sins that a revolving door may need to be fitted for me and that I could whiz round a few times every day for three days. We visited the statue of St James that you hug and put your head on and I said a few words and then it was off down to the crypt. This was what the pilgrimage was and no one was there so I kneeled before St James remains and I thanked him. I said a few other words and I thought that it was a very special place and I have no doubt we had some laughs along the way and he looked over me. Thank you, St James.

It was amazing and later that day I watched my new friend Sandrux do the same before we headed to the pilgrim's mass. As I waited for the mass to start I sat and smiled. Five hundred miles and every step was a lesson, a smile, a tear. My heart had taken me here and now I would sit back and listen before heading out with everyone for dinner. It's hard to describe the greatness of the feelings I felt. Life it's absolutely ours if we choose.

The mass was indeed a grand affair and we had taken our seats in the section at the front specially reserved for pilgrims. We were an hour early and when Pilgrims mass started I understood why we had been told to go early. This huge cathedral was packed and had TVs situated about it to beam live around the place what was happening at the huge and quite spectacular golden altar that had St James situated right in the centre. There was music and a procession of priests that led a visiting Cardinal to the altar and a nun who seemed to be the master of ceremonies conducted the worshipping audience in song and when to stand and sit. The whole thing, apart from one small section, was in Spanish and I had not a clue what was being said but this was the "Pilgrims Mass", a special mass, dedicated especially to us pilgrims so I enjoyed every bit of it. I just sat there and took it all in. Spectacular stuff whether you're religious or not. The mass continued for just over an hour and it came time for those who wanted to take communion. People waited in line and slowly moved forward one by one. The Irish people I knew slowly walked passed and Aodan, the funny Irish chap, just looked at me, smiled and said (think of thick Irish accent) "come on you ya big Protestant you, come and take some although you might burn" I burst out laughing and he chuckled as he moved forward. The mass had finished, and as it's a holy year, every Friday they swing the "big ball" as people seemed to call it but its name is the "Botafumeiro" which is a giant incense burner originally used to fumigate the stinking and disease ridden pilgrims. They lit this and a group of six or seven men hoisted this up and with a bell ringing like motion they got the burner swinging in a huge arc across the cathedral. It was spectacular stuff as it whisked across and over the masses of pilgrims and others there to see. Again, I was happy that my timing to see this was perfect and leaving the mass I reflected on the countless pilgrims who had attended the very same mass for centuries.

We all met up and went to a bar where countless stories were told and favourite parts of the Camino were explained in funny detail and we all laughed a lot. The stories were great and we were all hungry so we went for a donnar kebab. This was great as it was a restaurant and you get your kebab served by waiters and it was delicious. I left and it was time to say goodbye to my Swedish friend Thomas. A great man who had spent many an hour on the Camino with me and then I said goodbye to the Australians who had also spent more than half the time with us. All tremendous people. The Australians were off to walk the Portuguese Camino from Porto back to Santiago. I thought that that would be an interesting walk. I walked back to the albergue on my own. My thoughts on how I had arrived here were strolling through my mind and I sat in the living room area and waited for the others to arrive. We sat and played with phones as others booked flights and yet others taught each other card games. It was late and eventually, way after midnight, I went to bed.

"I choose to make the rest of my life, the best of my life." ~ Louise Hay

Back - Tiger, Lena, me, Iain, Elea, Alexandro, Aodan, Middle - Chelsea, Madii  Front - Eduardo, Thomas, Trish and Ciara

# 2nd April
I eat you – farewell my friend
Santiago de Compostela

When I woke this morning, everyone was still in bed and it was kind of dark. I could tell people were awake and after going to the toilet I returned and made the joke that anyone awake could go back to sleep as there was no walking today. There was a couple of tired giggles however it was not entirely true. Lena our German friend was heading to Finisterre which is another short Camino that pilgrims take to the sea and is about 100km. They thought it was the end of the world. Lena was a quiet girl and lovely girl with a beautiful look and quirky fun personality who became great friends with the Priest especially and it was great to have her walk with us. She was ready and with hugs from everyone and a last selfie another one of the group was gone. I lay in bed all morning and we all chatted and people came and went. The priest was going to be leaving and go to Barcelona however he had changed his mind and was going to walk to the end of the world also. He would not leave till lunchtime he said.

I booked an apartment as I wanted a couple of nights of luxury and it wasn't too expensive so I set off at around 11 and the

Yanks could have the sofa bed if they wanted so they came also and Eduardo, while not coming, said he'd have a space on the floor. The apartment was beautiful and had everything in it and the man who owns it could not have been more helpful. The girls were happy and I knew that the Mexican and German could have that bed after the girls left tomorrow. I must admit it would still be nice to have people around.

As we were getting into the apartment though we got a message from Eduardo to say that he was leaving with the priest soon. We didn't expect that so we set off to the meeting point. They were ready to go and I could feel the lump in my throat building when Eduardo got up to smile and say good bye. This was a tough one for me as Eduardo and I had met at the train station over 5 weeks earlier and we had become great friends and we laughed a lot. With a tear in my eye I embraced my friend. I will miss Italy.

The priest then arrived and we said our goodbyes to him and Tiger the priest is another person I will miss. A great guy who has a wicked sense of humour and is off to the army for two years before the priest bit. It was a pleasure to walk with both these guys and just like that and with a dance they were off. An hour later I received a video to say they were lost that made me laugh.

We headed for lunch and the mood was a little sad. We ate and all went to do things. I purchased some earphones and had a walk around the city reflecting. It was time to go for a nap. My body wanted it and so did my mind. The girls slept and so did I. It was bliss. Waking up just before five and looking outside at the pouring rain it was soon decided that we were not wanting to go out walking so I contacted Alexandro and Elea to see if they wanted to come over for dinner and they said yes.

The USA x 2 were going to cook and our friend Sandrux said she would come to have dinner also. I was pleased that we had the group together and as they cooked a beautiful pasta, a glass of wine was poured for them all and the talk was great. I lay on the bed and couldn't help but smile at my remaining Camino friends just relaxing and enjoying being together. The brief sadness of the parting of friends was lifted as I remembered that new friends and experiences are always just around the corner. These friends were forever though and I wouldn't forget them. They were a huge part of my Camino. From the Theologist and the Italian, to the Basque Princess, from Australia to Germany and the USA. The list goes on and Korea will entertain while the English will use their wit. Sweden will play music and Ireland will make jokes. What can I say about the people on the Camino other than I love my new friends.

The night and day had delivered emotions that I expected. People really can change and make people happy. Everyone has the power to deliver happiness. I witnessed it every day and I hoped I had delivered a little in return. Thoughts of friends I said goodbye to.

## AS WE ALL PART

Shared dreams, walking apart
Different directions, are we smart
Thoughts of each other, wondering, watching, waiting
Can the dreams be real

Finding work, yet not with vigour
Creating things, life is bigger
Looking out from far away, worried, ready, wanting
Closed eyes and imagination

Heads on pillows, room alone
Eyes wide open, you can not moan
Embrace the feelings, happy, content, proud
Dreams come true

~ Iain McKie

# 3rd April
## It's all about the people
## Santiago de Compostela

I fell asleep and I slept well. The noise of the girls' alarm going off in the distance, that was either real life or the new part of an amazing dream, helped bring my eyes and mind into a semi-conscious state and I checked the time. 7.30am. I would push my face a little deeper into the pillow for five minutes.

It's 8am and my eyes opened and thought you need to get to the shop to buy eggs so these girls have food before they leave. The girls were starting to rise and get ready and I headed off to the shop wondering if it would be open. The chances were slim as it was, first of all, Spain and my experience of opening times were a mystery not unlike the creation of the universe. It was also a Sunday that meant the above mystery was multiplied tenfold. My suspicion was correct and I was the only person walking down the street in the rain. Sunday mornings have their own feeling no matter where you are in the world I thought. I'm not sure I always enjoy the Sunday morning feeling.

The girls were ready to go and were getting a Bla Bla car back to Bilbao in northern Spain where they are studying. This transport idea is when you basically hitch a lift with someone and give them a small payment. It's all online and you have a profile etc. A great idea. The girls were singing then saying they didn't want to go back then singing again as they chatted about their dreams and soon we were all walking to the pickup place where the twenty-four-year-old guy would be waiting. We stopped off at a cafe and I bought them omelettes to make sure they were fed and we laughed when we received a message from Eduardo to say the others were already walking and he was in bed. The funny part being he then sent a message to Tiger and Lena, who were already walking, asking what town the albergue was in he was meant to go to. Lost again but still smiling. We set off through the ever so quiet streets of Santiago de Compostela and we were soon at the place to meet the guy. It turned out that it was two young girls that were taking my friends home and I was happy it was all coming together for their trip back but again I had to say goodbye to two amazing young people who embrace life. I had only known them for a short time but felt a great bond and somehow responsible for making sure they were ok. They called me uncle Iain and in some way, I guess I was. A group hug and some last-minute advice from me about always making sure the person in the mirror is happy and they were off towards the car. I was going to wait and wave but I couldn't. My emotions were starting to take over again and I put my music on and headed off to walk. Well just walk. I shed a tear of happiness for my friends and I knew that they would have many more adventures. I'll miss them.

I walked through the streets. They were quiet and I had a chance to start to take in this magnificent old town with its grandeur buildings surrounding the building that protects St James. My thoughts were deep and happy. I thought about what my next chapter would be like. One thing I knew was it would be a lot better than the last one. Maybe that had all been the introduction and the story of my life was now starting. What an exciting thought and I smiled as I stood in front of the cathedral. I took a picture for a newly arrived group of pilgrims and wondered what stories have walked through the archway and tunnel on to this historic plaza. A million pieces of heartache I'm sure was buried right under my feet as people let things go when they arrived. This place saved lives.

I went for a walk and ran into Lee. Lee was a Korean guy who started in St Jean also and walked the first few days with us. It was nice to see him and that's when a group of kids walked by singing at the top of their lungs and dancing. A school group, I presumed. That made me smile. I walked more and got a small memento and headed back to the apartment where a few minutes later I received a text from the theologist to say Elea and he were on their way over.

The three of us went to the pilgrim museum which was just quite fantastic. It showed pilgrimages from all over the world and for all the different reasons that people do them. It was over three floors and I could have spent a long time there. After this we went and ate. Then went to a coffee place that has been open for over one hundred years that was very posh. Ice cream coffee was lovely and Lee joined us. I was excited though as Luise my German friend was in town and we were going to meet up again. I had missed Luise so it would be great to see her again and off we went to meet her. After many hugs and hellos, we went to a bar to have a beer then it was back to the apartment where I cooked dinner and we all ate and they drank wine. It was great again to have my friends around and we talked and talked about the Camino and showed pictures. I read my poem and that was emotional. I was with true friends and I missed the ones who had moved on. My friend Eduardo was sick and we were hoping he would be ok. My last night of the Camino and St James is delivering me a present of being around my friends. I'm going to find it hard to say goodbye to these people. That's not till tomorrow though. Tonight, I will enjoy listening and telling stories. These last days have all been about the friends I have made. I feel truly blessed.

> "If you ask me how long I'll be your friend? My answer will be, I don't know., cause I really don't know which one is longer. FOREVER or ALWAYS?"

# 4th April

The last entry
Santiago de Compostela to home

This will be the last entry of this part of my life adventure and I know there will be more.

My final night was spent with three of the most amazing people I have met in my life. Elea the wife of the theologist, the theologist Alexandro and my beautiful German friend Luise. Luise had checked into an albergue however after some chat it was decided she would stay at the apartment and Alex and Elea would also. We all put our boots on and headed out into the cool evening air that Santiago de Compostela was offering and walked to collect Luise's rucksack. We chatted about all things Camino and we were all thankful that we could spend the last night together. Luise was the first person I walked with and it was nice that she was going to be one of the last as we collected her things. Alex, Elea and I had been together the whole time except the first day. These two had walked the Camino with me and are very special people. So here I was with these three and we bought some food and in the apartment they drank some wine and we talked. It was soon bedtime and the Camino is funny as you have to sleep where you have to sleep and Luise got the bed with me. A chore this Camino I thought. We did joke about it however I had already slept with the priest, the Spanish guy, Thomas the Swede and the unnamed Canadian woman to name a few so having a cute German girl next to me was nothing.

Luise was asleep in minutes, as were the other two but I was not going to get any sleep. I lay and listened to countless songs and I drifted in and out as I looked at the clock one last time well after 4am. I had lain there just happy that I had spent the last night with these guys and my mind raced with the adventure I was on when I must have fallen asleep. The alarm buzzed just after 7am. The first alarm I had set since leaving home and I got up to enjoy the shower one last time. When I came back into the room the others were waking up and I knew I'd soon be gone. I thanked them for just being them and Alex called a taxi for me. In no time the taxi was there which was good as it didn't give me too much time to get emotional but me being me it was still just enough for me to embrace my friends through some happy tears and with a Buen Camino and smiles I was waving at them from the open taxi window. I know I'll see them all again someday I thought. How could you not when you build such a good relationship.

To the airport I went when I realised I had forgotten something and I laughed. Just as I did I received a message from Luise to ask if I had left anything. My reply was yes, my earphones were my last offering to the Camino gods. Three sets I had lost but these ones would play music to one of my friends. The Camino gods work in mysterious ways as I laughed and wondered how I could invent earphones that were attached to your ear. Soon I was at the airport and checking my bag in. A friend Hannah had said do not take any selfies in the airport so I thought that I'd do it on the plane. I ate some breakfast and as I thought of the Camino it was mostly the people I thought about and I thanked St James again who I truly believe was, and still is, keeping an eye on me. I wouldn't have said that five weeks ago. I feel we are friends.

The flight was fine and I dosed and thought of the weeks and started thinking of what I was going to do now I was coming back to reality. Or was I leaving reality and coming back to unreality where unrealistic demands are asked of us and where that feeling of pure freedom you have on the Camino slowly ebbs away like the midnight tide. I decided I'd ensure I worked on that very scenario and not forget the feelings I've had.

I spent the time in London having a snack and then it was the short flight up to Glasgow and I was looking forward to seeing pops. His enthusiasm when talking to him when away helped me daily. It gave me that bit of extra energy sometimes just when I needed it. One thing about passing through three airports after the Camino was I was extremely proud to show off my shell and Camino t-shirt. In Londonm two people said

Buen Camino to me and I answered in Spanish of course. I loved it.

I arrived in Glasgow and surprisingly it wasn't raining and it was 9c which was much warmer than many of the days I had in northern Spain. How many people can fly in to Glasgow from Spain and say it's warmer here. A low percentage I'd say however it made me laugh. I called pops and he was waiting and it was great to see his smiling face and we headed back to Dunoon and went for dinner in Rio's where I ate pizza and it was beautiful. The conversation was pretty much all Camino and it was nice to be back with pops chatting and then it was home. My pilgrimage was complete.

*My Pops meeting me in Glasgow*

# To finish

It is impossible for me to capture the feelings and emotion I have right now as it's hard to contemplate the pilgrimage I have done even though I have the pictures to prove it. It was a day by day achievement with some incredible highs and not really any lows. If I had pain I knew I could get to a goal and rest as I did when I was sick. The people around me came together every day to share the experience. No one judged and everyone had a story. There was routine in the day in that you woke up, you walked, you ate and then you slept. The basic of life's needs such as food and water were part of your planning and the smallest of everyday things that you are used to at home became an incredible luxury. Hot water to wash and a towel. Oh how I appreciate a regular bath towel now. Every decision had an effect to your goal of reaching Santiago and while some seemed trivial every one of them was important. Many were mistakes or wrong decisions but these just helped you even more as you travelled along the Camino. You learned to ask for things and help in various languages and relied on the help of others in situations and helped people whenever you could. Nature and towns were no longer just something you passed through they were acutely something you felt and my mind was out looking and listening all the time at what was around me and danced with joy at the things it was seeing and hearing. Daily you met incredible people and daily I was thinking and contemplating not just life but my life. It was incredible.

What's next people have asked. I don't know is the honest answer. I look forward to seeing my dad and friends and then who knows, the book, the screenplay, the movie, the art exhibition and the poetry book, the garden, the hills to walk, the other Caminos and the Appellation Trail or maybe I'll walk the Pacific coast in the U.S. .... The list is infinite and I know that along whatever path I choose that I'll do it trying hard to deliver happiness to others and myself.

I want to say a huge thank you to all who have read this and commented or sent me messages. These inspired me. Thank you to pops and my friends who, if they doubted, never showed it and supported me the entire way. Dad I know I've made you proud. Thank you to the wonderful people I met on The Camino and the close close friends who, when I think of them, my heart will always smile. Last of all I'd like to thank myself for being brave enough to ask for help when needed and started taking risks that have rewarded me with happiness and love. I'm missing someone – ah, of course my friend St James. Thank you again for listening to it all and guiding me.

Life is a beautiful thing that sometimes I just didn't see.
I didn't look hard enough in the mirror at the great person
who was just waiting to be seen.
I feared I don't know what.
I ask every one of you who has been kind enough to read this
to take a look in the mirror
and find the amazing person staring back at them.
There right there and they love you.
Give them a chance.

## This is your life

Thank you all and of course
**Buen Camino**

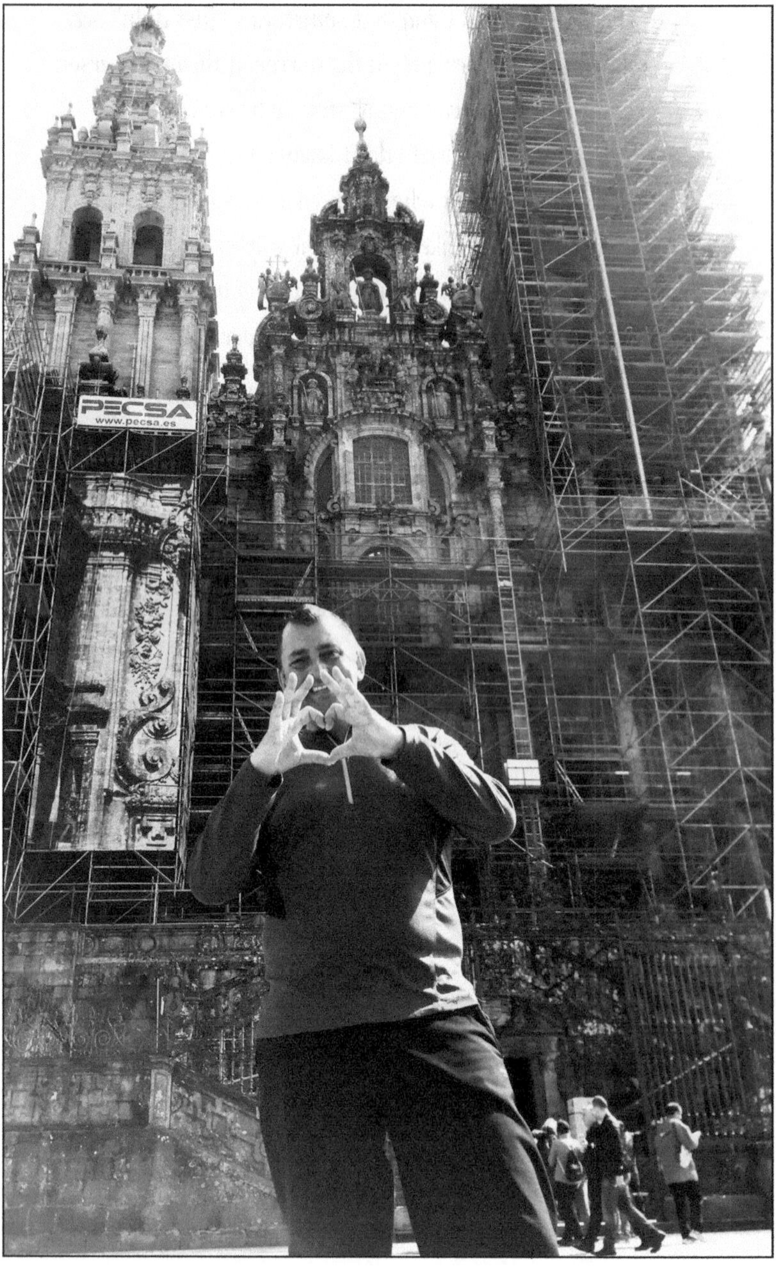
PECSA
www.pecsa.es

Scruffy Red Publishing
Kilmarnock, Scotland (c) 2017